THE WORLD ACCORDING TO
DEAN

Four Decades of Basketball
as Seen by Dean Smith

★ ★ ★

THE WORLD ACCORDING TO

DEAN

**Four Decades of Basketball
as Seen by Dean Smith**

by
Barry Jacobs

TOTAL
SPORTS

New York

Published by
Total Sports, Inc.
445 Park Avenue, 19th Floor
New York, New York 10022

Distributed by
Andrews McMeel Publishing
Distribution Center
PO Box 419150
Kansas City, Missouri 64141

For information about permission to reproduce selections from this
book, please write to:
Permissions
Total Sports, Inc.
105 Abeel Street
Kingston, New York 12401

Total Sports™ is a trademark of Total Sports, Inc.

Interior Design: Sherry Williams

Library of Congress Catalog Card Number: 98-87943

ISBN 0-9656949-8-4

Printed in U.S.A.

Book produced by
Balliett & Fitzgerald, Inc.
Additional editorial material by: Rob Daniels

Photo Credits:
Robert Crawford; 18 32, 56, 59, 64, 65, 73, 86, 87, 92, 97, 102, 105,
106, 121.

Bob Donnon; 13, 16, 20, 22, 23, 25, 27, 45, 46, 48, 62, 78, 80, 83, 85,
89, 109, 110, 112, 115, 117, 119, 120

Hugh Morton; 12, 24, 29, 35, 36, 39, 42, 52, 54, 60, 63, 66, 68, 69,
70, 75, 76-77, 84, 90, 99, 101, 114

■

To Dean Smith,

a credit to the teaching profession,

and to Robin,

one of his greatest admirers.

■

ACKNOWLEDGEMENTS

Much of the material in this book comes from interviews I conducted with Dean Smith or from press conferences I attended over 20 years, most often for *The New York Times* or *The Fan's Guide To ACC Basketball*.

Smith tends to express himself in incomplete sentences, sometimes jumping between subjects and decades without warning. "My mind gets ahead of what I'm saying," Smith says. "I think that's common among math-aptitude types." So thanks to Dagmar Cooley, Anne Hastings, Susan Morris, Dan Pelletier, John Royster, Lydia Wheeler, and Barbara White for their diligence in transcribing the coach's comments.

Many of the same people, as well as Tony Britt, assisted in the collection of articles detailing Smith's views. Further research assistance was kindly provided by the sports information staff at the University of North Carolina.

Indispensible editorial guidance was provided by Vijay Balakrishnan, Will Balliett, Liz Barrett, and Sue Canavan. Sherry Williams contributed a graceful design. Support of a more basic sort was extended by the folks at Total Sports, most especially John Thorn, Donna Harris, Frank Daniels III, and George Schlukbier.

No project of this magnitude can be accomplished without encouragement from generous friends like Julian King, Eddy Landreth, Bernice Jacobs, Gary Rosenthal, and the Moorefields dog contingent—Adams, Jefferson, Sparky, Ted, Tyler, Millie, Ford, and Truman.

And always there's Robin, my wife, to smooth out the rough edges, read the draft text, and help keep things in perspective.

—BJ

The World According to Dean

C O N T E N T S

FOREWORD

by
Roy Williams

In writing this foreword, I have contrasting emotions. First of all I am flattered because of what Coach Smith means to me. I am not unusual in that respect, since all of his former players and coaches would love the opportunity to praise him publicly. On the other hand, I realize that he doesn't like such tributes and doesn't want anybody to spend any time talking about him. But since he has given his blessing to my writing this foreword, I'm more than delighted to take this rare opportunity.

As I spent time thinking about what to write, I considered discussing Coach's faults before his strengths. That would probably be more comfortable for him because it would be more balanced. The problem with this plan is that Dean Smith's actual faults would be great strengths for anyone else. I think Coach Smith is *too* loyal. I think he gives too much of himself and his time and his finances to his former players and coaches. He is continually giving because his loyalty is unconditional and has no limits. So, in fact, that fault is truly a strength. Coach has said that he doesn't have the patience he needs to have and yet I think that "lack of patience" actually shows up as a drive and a push for excellence in others. I think he is patient. He provided an explanation to his players and expected them to do it, and that in turn pushed them even more. So much for his faults.

I feel a truly great leader is a person who doesn't have to treat everyone the same. He can treat people differently and they will understand because he is going to be fair with all of them. In the ten years I was with Coach as an assistant, I felt he was tougher on Michael Jordan than on any other player we ever had. He chose to push Michael so hard because he saw something special in him that needed to be challenged. Coach chooses the best way to work with each and every individual.

When I think of Coach Smith, what comes to mind is his competitiveness. I love to play golf, I love to think I am a good putter, and I love to think I am competitive. But if I were ever allowed to pick someone to putt a six-footer for the win, it would have to be Dean Smith. Not because he's the greatest putter, but because he's the greatest competitor, and he would find a way to get it in.

In addition, his organizational skills and his ability to focus on the important details are really gifts. He has the ability to inspire people to make tremendous sacrifices and have them feel like it's their choice. His greatest strength, then, is his true love and care for the people who work with him and for the players who have played for him.

So many times I am asked about "what Coach is really like." I always give the proper answer—the truth—and I always feel that people are just shaking their heads and saying, "He can't be that good." In actuality, he is so, so much better. The degree of his love for the University of North Carolina, and for all the players and coaches there, truly sets him apart from everyone else. His intelligence, his passion and loyalty for his players and staff, and his single-mindedness in attempting to achieve a goal are the essence of the man.

He has meant so much to me that it is impossible to put into words. He truly is a man that you can not describe. He is only a man that you can love. Thank you Coach for everything you have meant to me and many, many others.

by
Barry Jacobs

The game and the season were over for the University of Washington. The Huskies had lost at the buzzer in the 1998 NCAA East Regional, failing to control a loose ball at the brink of breakthrough success.

As the postgame crush eased, a friend approached Bob Bender and congratulated the Washington coach on his team's performance. Bender said his thanks and headed for a last interview. Two strides later the former Duke player and assistant coach paused, and then turned, smiling ruefully.

"As Coach Smith would say," Bender told the friend, "it was a great college basketball game if you didn't care who won."

However pained, the remark touched on a real truth about college basketball. In a hundred ways large and small, the personality and philosophies of Dean Edwards Smith permeate the game, shaping the way we watch it and how it's played.

For 36 years, starting in 1961, Smith was head coach at the University of North Carolina; his widely mimicked nasal twang, eyebrows winged like Mercury's feet, and fierce appetite for control were as integral to the game as orange rims. Before the 40-year-old Bender was a teenager, Smith's Tar Heels had emerged as a national power. By the time Bender enrolled in college, UNC was a fixture at the game's summit, having embarked on a run of consecutive trips to the NCAA Tournament that continues to this day.

"North Carolina has had the best college basketball program of the last generation," says Jim Boeheim, the highly successful head coach at Syracuse.

To inventory Smith's influence, start with the jump-switch or the scramble defense, the secondary break or the passing offense. Move on to the Four Corners delay or the science of clock management: how coaches manipulate end-game situations with deliberate fouling, juggled timeouts, and substitutions. Watch players huddle at the foul line, point to teammates to credit an assist, or raise a fist to request a breather. Discuss the merits of freshman ineligibility or the right of players to leave college early to join the pros. Listen to a coach wax absurd to downplay his team, damn an opponent with faint praise, or take the long view to rationalize a defeat. Contemplate raising consistency to an art form and victory and control to relentless habits.

Do all that, and you get a sense of Smith's imprint on the game.

Basketball is little more than a century old, conjured by James Naismith in 1891. But as the game has evolved from a partially segregated and rarely televised pastime to an international affair under constant scrutiny, no figure has been more central than Smith.

By the time Smith retired in 1997, his Carolina teams had won 879 games, giving him more victories than any major-college coach. In the process his Tar Heels were more consistently excellent—averaging better than 24 wins per year, appearing in postseason play in each of his last 31 seasons, and winning two national titles—than any program except John Wooden's UCLA colossus of the 1960s and early 1970s.

Smith's former players, led by the incomparable Michael Jordan, crowd lists of All-Americans and all-pros. Rules for which Smith lobbied, most notably the three-point basket and the shot clock, changed the shape of college ball. His squads set high standards for discipline, selflessness and efficiency on the court. Teams at every level of basketball run North Carolina plays and embrace Smith's meticulously honed defensive and offensive schemes.

All this was achieved without hint of scandal or player abuse, and nearly all of Smith's recruits went on to graduate with meaningful degrees. Players to whom Smith offered a teacher's guiding hand became part of an enduring, extended family. Smith set aside part of every Monday to take calls from some of his 200 former players, assistants, and student-managers, freely offering assistance and advice in matters personal and professional.

"It's really a simple thing that some people try to make a complicated thing," says Bill Guthridge, who served at Smith's side for 30 years and succeeded him as UNC head coach in October of 1997. "He's just a very smart, intelligent, caring person. And his occupation is a basketball coach, and he's very good at it. He's got a few close friends, but he's no gladhander. He really cares about his former players—their jobs, their families—and the players in school."

Smith was so good at his job—his teams finished no lower than third in the Atlantic Coast Conference from 1965 through 1997, and finished first 17 times—that he forced opponents to elevate their play merely to keep pace. That in turn propelled the ACC to its current status as the nation's most balanced and perennially powerful league.

Beating North Carolina became a goal in itself for conference rivals. "I thought it was Naismith who invented the game, not Dean Smith," griped one ACC coach.

Actually, not so far from the truth, given that Smith does trace his basketball roots directly to Naismith. The inventor of the game was also the first head coach at the University of Kansas and Smith, who was born in Emporia, Kansas, on February 28, 1931, went on to play for Naismith's successor at Kansas, Forrest "Phog" Allen, attending on an academic scholarship with the intention of becoming a high school math teacher and coach.

Smith's parents, Kansas natives Vesta and Alfred Smith, were teachers and active Baptists who worked to instill in their offspring a tolerant faith. Vesta Smith interrupted her career to stay in the family's stucco house a few blocks from downtown Emporia until her two children reached junior high, first daughter Joan and then son Dean, named after one of his mother's favorite teachers. Alfred Smith coached basketball, football, track, and baseball at Emporia High. His basketball team won the state title shortly after his son was born, but he was expelled from the Kansas coaches' association for using black players.

Young Dean Smith hung around the gym and the playing fields, learning the game from the inside, and later played decision-making positions in football (quarterback), baseball (catcher), and basketball (point guard). Offered a partial scholarship to Kansas State, he chose instead to attend Kansas, where his father had earned a master's degree.

The 5'-10" guard spent two years on Allen's varsity, and was a "cagey little operator," according to the 1953 Kansas media guide. Smith, a dependable ballhandler and adept defender, was the third guard on the 1952 team that, led by All-American Clyde Lovellette, finished 28-3 and won the NCAA championship. As a senior, Smith played in every game on a 19-6 squad that again reached the national title game.

"He was a skillful player, as he is a skillful coach," said Dick Harp, an assistant on those Kansas teams, "and he was a creative player, just as he is a creative coach."

Following graduation, Smith spent a year assisting Allen and Harp at Kansas while working at a nearby gypsum plant and playing on its AAU team. He then went to Germany to fulfill an Air Force ROTC commitment. Soon Captain Smith was transferred to Colorado, where he assisted Bob Spear for three years (1955-56 to 1957-58) at the newly opened Air Force Academy. Spear then recommended him to Frank McGuire, the North Carolina coach.

Like Smith's first mentor, Phog Allen, McGuire had won a national title (at North Carolina in 1957) and became a member of the Naismith Basketball Hall of Fame. Smith immediately impressed the flamboyant New Yorker with his organizational abilities and defensive strategies. "Dean has it figured out pretty mathematically," McGuire said.

Although his playing days were over, Smith was wound so tight that, while still asleep, he'd leap out of bed on road trips and strike the defensive stances ingrained by Allen. "Once he shouted at me," McGuire said of his young roommate. "I almost went through the ceiling."

When North Carolina's men's basketball team incurred NCAA and university sanctions in 1961, McGuire departed for the NBA. He recommended Smith as his successor. The chancellor agreed, and the 30-year-old became head coach the same year John Kennedy was inaugurated and the Berlin Wall went up separating East from West Germany.

Smith's first Carolina team was 8-9, his only losing record. Trouble came three seasons later. Well into the 1964-65 season, the Tar Heels' modest performance sparked such dissatisfaction that Smith was twice hanged in effigy on campus. Throughout his career, Smith recalled those unhappy days as a turning point in his ability to keep winning and losing in perspective.

Two seasons later, Dean Smith took the Tar Heels to the 1967 Final Four. They went for three straight years, and four times in six seasons. Suddenly Smith was a hero, growing to near-icon status among North Carolina fans.

But as his success grew, Smith was careful to deflect attention, and limit access to himself, his program, and his players. Critics denounced this as authoritarian, image-conscious control.

Image was important to Smith, who rarely chastised a player in public and never cursed (according to all but a handful of opponents). Back when he chain smoked Kent cigarettes—he quit during the fall of 1988 after experiencing several days of nosebleeds—he hid from TV cameras while indulging. Even amidst summer's stickiest heat, Smith and his staff wore long pants on the recruiting trail, and at games he dressed with a businessman's decorum.

"People talk about our image and make it sound contrived," Smith said in the mid-1970s. "We want to represent the university well. Simple things like manners and wearing a coat and tie everywhere, they blend in with playing unselfishly. I don't think we've ever embarrassed the school, and that's tremendously important to me."

Yet, loyalty to his school didn't prevent Smith from pushing to further social values he considered important.

Long before racial reconciliation became a common goal, particularly in the segregated South, Smith broke a color barrier by accompanying his pastor, Robert Seymour, and a black theology student to a restaurant in Chapel Hill. Smith also began recruiting black players when he became head coach. He courted Greensboro's Lou Hudson, an eventual all-pro, and later signed Willie Cooper, who quit basketball in 1965 to concentrate on academics. That left Charles Scott to become the first African-American player on UNC's varsity in 1967-68.

Smith's beliefs also eventually led him to demonstrate against the Vietnam War, do ads for a nuclear freeze, oppose the death penalty, and support his Chapel Hill church's inclusion of female and gay ministers.

For all the coach's sense of proportion, the demands of the job took their toll, mortally wounding his first marriage. "The divorce was the most traumatic thing I have ever been through," Smith said of the his 1973 split with Anne, with whom he had had two daughters and a son. Several years later he married Linnea Koning, a psychiatrist with whom he had two daughters.

And as his fame grew, Smith assiduously guarded his privacy. He eschewed most commercial endorsements, stuck to back-rooms at Chapel Hill restaurants, and asked friends to decline reporters' interview requests. After the Tar Heels won the 1982 national title, defeating Georgetown, 63-62, Smith went as far as to refuse all interviews focused on himself.

Before that victory, criticism of Dean Smith centered on his program's inability to capture an NCAA championship. Six times he had taken a team to the Final Four without winning, a failure widely attributed to a style that supposedly sacrificed individuality in the name of the whole, stressing conformity to the point that Tar Heel players were interchangeable parts, near-faceless robots.

Smith bristled at such characterizations, claiming he nurtured flexibility and freedom within necessary parameters. He was so sensitive on this subject, that when UNC finally won in '82, Smith opened his postgame press conference by chiding a writer from Charlotte who had claimed the "system" prevented individuals from rising to an occasion, thus dooming the Tar Heels to ultimate failure.

Smith's retort reflected a relentless competitive fire that burned fiercely whether on the sidelines, the golf course, or during an interview. That competitiveness never waned, and by the time Smith retired, the Tar Heels had been to 11 Final Fours. Only Wooden took more teams to the national semifinals (12), and no other coach took teams to the Final Four in four different decades, as Smith did.

North Carolina reached the final game five times. The 1982 Georgetown victory muted talk that Smith was a choker. A 77-71 defeat of Michigan in 1993 gave Smith his second title and diffused claims that the game had passed him by.

The Heels' presence in the NCAAs became as common a part of Carolina spring as dogwood blossoms and returning robins. Under Smith, Carolina won 65 NCAA tournament games, appeared 27 times, and earned 23 straight bids. All are records. (See Deanology, p.120, for a more complete breakdown of Smith's career statistics.)

Smith's teams also produced 10 consensus All-Americans—Larry Miller, Bob McAdoo, Phil Ford, James Worthy, Michael Jordan, Sam Perkins, Kenny Smith, J.R. Reid, Jerry Stackhouse, and Antawn Jamison—and 26 NBA first-round

draft choices. Eight of the nine UNC players who left school early to enter the NBA were chosen in the draft's opening round. And six former Tar Heels, more than any other school, have had their jerseys retired by NBA franchises—Billy Cunningham (Philadelphia), Brad Daugherty (Cleveland), Walter Davis (Phoenix), Bobby Jones (Philadelphia), Jordan (Chicago), and Worthy (L.A. Lakers).

But while attracting an array of outstanding players was a key to Smith's success, so was what he taught them after they arrived.

Smith enveloped players in a framework that stressed communal effort, and enforced discipline to achieve it. Student-managers charted every play in summer pickup games. Each movement at practice and games was videotaped and critiqued, even bench behavior. Until players proved themselves as students, assistant coaches followed them to class to check their attendance.

Practices were run with a precision the military would envy, stressing fundamentals and preparation. "I don't think there's a situation that occured in my four years that we hadn't practiced before," said Ged Doughton, who played at UNC from 1976-79.

In fact, to bring home the importance of communal effort, North Carolina rendered statistics alphabetically and without denoting starters or playing time. The offense worked to get the best shot available no matter who took it. When you played the Tar Heels you ran into a team that stressed intelligence and defense, always played hard and competed against their own high standards rather than specific opponents.

By the early 1980s UNC had been so successful, that speculation arose that Smith would eclipse the 876 wins achieved by Kentucky's Adolph Rupp, another former Kansas player under Allen. Soon Smith let it be known that he'd retire or resign rather than achieve the record.

Uttering dismissive comments all the way, Smith finally got his 877th career win on March 15, 1997, a 73-56 defeat of Colorado in the second round of the NCAA Tournament. UNC won twice more, sending Smith to his 11th Final Four, before the season ended. Then, on the eve of preseason practice the following October, Smith abruptly retired.

"I have gotten too much attention, and maybe that is a part of why I am doing this," Smith said with his characteristic determined modesty at a press conference in the building that bears his name. "I enjoy basketball. I enjoy coaching basketball. It's the out-of-season things I haven't been able to handle very well."

Now Smith limits his competition mostly to golf, and his basketball activity to observation, teaching, and advice. But that doesn't mean that every time you attend or watch a college basketball game you don't see Dean Smith. You do. In a hundred different ways.

Bench huddle in 1996

CHAPTER 1

The Game of Basketball

"**I consider Dean Smith's 36-year record one of the great accomplishments in the history of sports. You can look at what coaches have done at the professional and college level in football, basketball, baseball, any sport, and his record stands alone.**"

—*Rick Barnes,*
current coach at Texas and
former coach at Clemson,
October 9, 1997

THE GAME OF BASKETBALL

June 1990:

"Beauty is in the eye of the beholder... I see one of our defenses come up and get a steal, I think that's pretty. It's fun to watch our old blue team come in and move the ball, move the ball, and all of a sudden someone goes back door and lays it in.

It's a game where you need to be very unselfish...."

September 1991:

"It's a beautiful game, (but) it's getting a little too physical....Television has changed it."

January 1990:

"It's gotten to the point where it's going to be a survival of the strongest, and it wasn't intended to be that way.... It should be dependent on finesse as much as strength."

North Carolina's bench made a point of acknowledging assists and other unselfish plays.

January 1972:

"Nine years ago, if I felt we had better personnel than the other team, I didn't think there was any way that we could lose. But I'm not that way now. I've seen it happen too many times, where the team that was supposed to be better didn't win. I rarely will pick up a newspaper and not find at least one score that surprises me. So, I believe experience tends to make us more cautious. I can remember when I never had any trouble making short putts. I was sure I could make them. But two or three years ago I missed a real easy three-footer. Now, I'm not so sure of myself. I know it's possible to miss them."

October 1991:
"Once we go out on the court, everybody's the same. Some are just better than others."

AWARDS

Smith was quick to lobby for awards for his players, though he insisted that individual achievement be judged within the context of team performance. He often was overlooked for national coaching honors, but he was ACC coach of the year eight times. No other coach has won the award more than three times.

March 1988:
"They don't have doctors of the year, lawyers of the year, whatever. I wish they didn't have coach, either. I think we all tend to be pretty consistent. That award never comes out right."

CHEMISTRY

December 1995:
"It comes and goes depending on who's happy."

June 1994:
"The best way to build team chemistry is the way Rupp used to substitute. When they fouled out."

July 1993 (Smith's 1993-94 squad was loaded with talent and ultimately undermined by it.):
"Our problem is we have too much depth.... If your last five can win games, then you really have trouble with chemistry."

March 1994:
"Most good teams play with about six people and develop chemistry. We've always done it with six or seven. That's going to be hard with this team, because someone is going to be sitting who thinks he should be playing more."

December 1992:

"The good teams don't have too much depth. The ideal team is eight guys who can play, and then the next five who would like to play and work hard in practice."

October 1994, on a loss in the 1994 NCAA tournament:

"Chemistry didn't have anything to do with our missing a few shots against Boston College."

COMEBACKS

For many years, the North Carolina media guide has devoted a section to improbable comebacks under Dean Smith. Usually there was at least one such rally per season. The quintessential Smith comeback occurred at Carmichael Auditorium on March 2, 1974. Despite playing with neither a shot clock nor a three-pointer, North Carolina rallied to a 96-92 overtime victory after trailing Duke by eight points with 17 seconds to go.

Tar Heels celebrated more than three victories for every defeat during Smith's career.

"No game's ever lost in the first half."

—December 1988

Pearce Landry, a walk-on, played a significant role on a 1995 squad that reached the Final Four.

January 1997 (In a stunning reversal of form, the Tar Heels squandered a 22-point lead with 14 and a half minutes to go, and lost to Maryland, 85-75.):
"The Maryland game was something we'll certainly remember. I'll remember when I'm sitting in a rocking chair."

January 1993, about a timeout called with 9:21 to go and UNC trailing by 17. (The Tar Heels went on to win by five.):
"I just thought at that time to let Florida State know, 'Uh, oh. Here we come. Timeouts.' I don't think it probably bothered them. And I wanted our players to know, okay, now we're in catch-up, and we're really going to get after them. And (there's) plenty of time, plenty of time. I brought up the Wake Forest game, when they came from that far back. And (the players) believed, I think. If they didn't believe, they believed when we got to 10."

DEDICATION

August 1980:
"We're talking about real artists by the time they get to this level. That means hours and hours and hours of practice. If you think of it, something has driven them— I don't know what it is—to get to this level."

August 1980:

"In order to spend that many hours (practicing) you have to have an almost neurotic need to excel."

Summer 1985, recalling guard Phil Ford in the fall of 1974:

"We do the mile run the first day of practice to check their conditioning. I remember someone was using this track, and we had to go to a cinder track. And Phil was coming down the line as a freshman. There were two of them, and he dives across the line. This guy wants it... (that's) an intangible you don't know in recruiting.... It's going beyond the point where you'd like to stop."

Phil Ford (left) and Walter Davis after winning the ACC Tournament

THE NBA DRAFT

Fifty-four men who played under Smith at North Carolina went on to careers in the American or National Basketball Association. Half of those were first-round NBA draft choices. Smith was known for maneuvering to get his players chosen by someone even if they were marginal prospects.

July 1993:

"I don't know who'll be a first-round draft pick. I have a lot more important things to worry about. I hope all of our guys are first-round. We would win all of our games and I could play golf."

June 1989:

"When Sam Perkins was a junior, a firm in Chicago sent a good-looking woman lawyer down here to try to get (him) as a client. He called me immediately, and told me what was going on. I told him to get out of his apartment and hide from her."

(PERKINS PLAYED AT UNC FROM 1981 TO '84, AND WAS ACTIVE IN THE NBA THROUGH THE 1997-98 SEASON.)

June 1996:

"Each year, there are three or four who you'd say, 'Hey, he really has to mess up not to make it to the next level,' but I'm talking about three or four. The only three I ever had, when they came in as freshmen (that) I thought were bound to be NBA players, the only three I could say with some certainty—not total—were James Worthy, Sam Perkins and Rasheed Wallace, because they had size, they had some skill, and they had speed and quickness. And attitude."

EXPECTATIONS

Smith's UNC teams were constantly at the top of the heap—among the best three in the ACC every season starting in 1965—and that level of success came to be simply expected, much to the coach's chagrin.

February 1975:

"It shows how far the program has progressed here that we finished eighth in the nation last year and were disappointed at the time."

> *"What boggles the mind about him, at least to me, are the numbers of nights he's gone into the arena and been ready to compete on every single possession. I've not done it anywhere close to half as often and there are nights it seems the season will never end. And yet, he's there, ready to go, always figuring out a way to beat you."*
>
> —Dave Odom,
> Wake Forest coach,
> on Dean Smith

February 1978:

"No matter how much I tell our players there is no real pressure to win a game, people on the street, newspapers, TVs and radios oppose that view. And, so, they feel they have to win."

February 1986:

"Some people say to me, 'Oh, we'll be happy as long as you keep bringing in fine young men to represent the university.' But I'd rather not test them by going 7-20."

March 1988:

"I've often said I'm only nervous before a game when we're playing somebody that's very good and my team thinks they'll beat them by 20."

DEFENSE

Aggressive, pressure defense was a North Carolina trademark through most of Smith's career. He was fond of changing defenses—sometimes within the same possession—in order to discomfit an opponent. Innovations such as the jump-switch and the scramble were attributed to Smith. Unlike most teams, Carolina also allowed opposing dribblers to attack along the baseline, where the Tar Heels trapped routinely. Inexperienced ballhandlers also were frequent targets of UNC traps. During the 1990s, as North Carolina squads had more size than quickness, Smith adjusted his thinking to suit his personnel, and his defensive strategy became less aggressive.

February 1988:
"Most of our thoughts are directed toward how we're going to stop the other team."

" No matter how somebody looks, if they can play a little defense, they'll do."
—March 1971

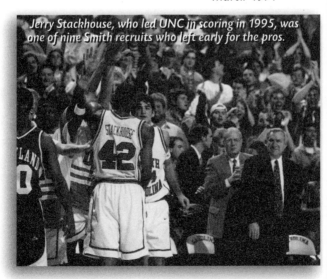

Jerry Stackhouse, who led UNC in scoring in 1995, was one of nine Smith recruits who left early for the pros.

February 1978:

"When we grade an individual's defensive performance, we do it on the basis of his execution of principles and not his man's scoring total."

January 1972:

"Actually, everything we do is based on man-to-man pressure. But we have a number of variations. We like to keep people wondering what we're going to do next... I got that idea from watching football. I noticed the offense would be trying to guess what kind of coverage the defense was in."

February 1978:

"(I believe in) change just for the sake of change. The defense dictates to the offense, forcing the other team to adjust, instead of the reverse. It's like the baseball pitcher who mixes in off-speed stuff with his fastball. It keeps the batter guessing."

March 1971:

"The offense will always have the advantage against a defense that just sits there waiting to be attacked, waiting for somebody to take a shot. So, if you're on defense, you've got to go get the ball."

March 1980:

"We believe in gambling a lot defensively, and it gets us a lot of easy shots on the other end, which is why our field goal percentage is always so high. On the other hand, the gambles don't always pay off so we'll give up a lot too. But it usually works out in our favor."

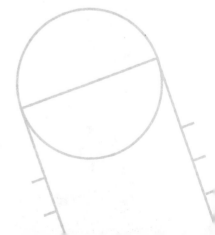

> # *" So much is talked about the offensive end. It's only half the game. "*
>
> *—December 1994*

April 1979, on the proposed addition of a 30-second shot clock:

"I would prefer it without zones, but I don't think the other conference coaches would go along with that. In my opinion, holding the ball and zones are both signs of weakness."

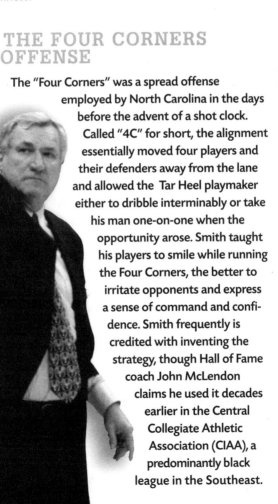

THE FOUR CORNERS OFFENSE

The "Four Corners" was a spread offense employed by North Carolina in the days before the advent of a shot clock. Called "4C" for short, the alignment essentially moved four players and their defenders away from the lane and allowed the Tar Heel playmaker either to dribble interminably or take his man one-on-one when the opportunity arose. Smith taught his players to smile while running the Four Corners, the better to irritate opponents and express a sense of command and confidence. Smith frequently is credited with inventing the strategy, though Hall of Fame coach John McLendon claims he used it decades earlier in the Central Collegiate Athletic Association (CIAA), a predominantly black league in the Southeast.

February 1973:

"I think everybody has always used a spread-out offense against a zone press. What we did that was unique occurred in 1963 while we were preparing for a game with Duke. We had Larry Brown, a real good ballhandler in the middle. During a practice, we told our defense to sneak into a straight man-to-man to see if Larry would recognize it and then go into a man-to-man delay. A funny thing happened. Larry didn't recognize it, but he drove by his man and laid the ball in the basket. The next time he drove in a corner a man came in to help defend, and Larry passed off to the open man, who laid it in the basket. It dawned on me that we could use the same delay against a man-to-man or zone or anything. It makes for a man-to-man situation and keeps them spread so they can't double-team you."

February 1978:

"When it works—about 90 percent of the time—you are a genius. When it fails, you're a bum."

November 1981:

"I don't like to talk about the Four Corners because so many people don't realize that the NCAA came out with a list of the highest scoring teams the last 10 years, and we were fourth on the list. We were averaging 84 points per game, so we believe in the fast break."

December 1988:

"Four Corners can't be what it once was, but it can still be useful."

"You didn't just play North Carolina; you played Dean Smith and the whole team."

—Maryland coach Gary Williams,
former Terrapin player,
October 9, 1997

FREE-THROW SHOOTING

Smith's teams usually were among the best in the ACC at the free throw line. Seven times they led the conference in foul shooting. During the 1990s North Carolina's acuity at the line was less consistent from year to year, and Smith preferred not to discuss it.

June 1989:
"The free throw is the common denominator whether there's 23,000 people or there's two people, or it's practice. It's the same person shooting the foul shots."

" The best offensive game is to get to the foul line."

—June 1994

June 1995:
"In all schoolyard games, I found over the years, you don't shoot foul shots. You're not practicing game-like conditions."

June 1985:
"One of my old jokes is, I had Donnie Walsh as a freshman, and he came in as a 68 percent foul shooter. And I worked with him and I got him up to 57 percent."
(DONNIE WALSH, THE SIX-FOOTER FROM RIVERDALE, N.Y., WHO PLAYED AT UNC FROM 1960 TO '62, HIT 54.8 PERCENT FROM THE FOUL LINE AS A VARSITY PLAYER.)

January 1996:
"One guy misses, then the next guy does, and pretty soon it's an epidemic."

June 1996:
"The only thing you can do is practice. You make them, you have good form. Then it becomes mental. You try to work on it, not talk about it."

REBOUNDING

February 1997:
"We spend more time on that than anything."

August 1982:
"If I get two shots to your every one, guess who wins?"

SHOOTING

January 1997:
"Anybody can be a good shooter. It's go out and practice it. I'm not sure kids do that anymore."

Action from win No. 877, versus Colorado in Winston-Salem

March 1984:
"You may be the best player on the team, but you don't take those risky falling-away-from-the basket, off-balance shots. You get it to somebody who can take a good shot. You shoot selfish shots, you sit down."

December 1995:
"It's easier to tell a guy to shoot than it is to tell him to stop shooting."

SUBSTITUTIONS

December 1972:
"We teach our men that a teammate is the most important thing. When we make a substitution, all our players stand up. I may be mad at the player, but I applaud... I will never embarrass a young man publicly."

THE THREE-POINTER

October 1993:

"You know how much I was fighting for the 3-point shot. If you're going to have the shot clock, then you've got to have the 3-pointer to go with it. It's amazing. Everybody got upset—'We're ruining the game'—and now everybody likes it."

December 1995:

"The 3-pointer is almost luck. I'm wondering how important the pressure is on a 3-point shot."

THE TIRED SIGNAL

March 1978:

"My first year as head coach, I was just 29—and scared to death. I told the team about the tired signal. Four or five times in the first half a player gave it to me. I thought they were saying, 'We're getting them, Coach.' I had forgotten my own signal."

November 1981:

"I'd rather have a fresh, enthusiastic player going for a short period than a tired player with more talent."

GUARDS

North Carolina point guards were expected to be extensions of Smith's will on the court. As such, they learned to anticipate his strategic decisions; the sooner they did so, the more they played.

June 1985:

"I always tell our point guards, it's like a quarterback who gets his team in the end zone. The quarterback who's going to play is the one who gets his team in the end zone the most, not the one who completes the most passes.... We don't know ahead of time for sure who is going to get the shot."

October 1996:

"In college... usually teams that are solid at the guard position are solid all the way around."

THE ATLANTIC COAST CONFERENCE

The ACC was founded in 1953 by eight schools that chose to abandon the sprawling Southern Conference. Of the original members, the so-called "Big Four"— Duke, UNC Chapel Hill, North Carolina State, and Wake Forest—were from North Carolina, where the league established its headquarters. Over the years the ACC earned a reputation as the nation's consistently strongest basketball league. Its teams have made it to the NCAA Final Four 29 times and won seven titles; no other league has had as many Final Four teams. Two or more ACC teams have reached the NCAA Tournament's Sweet 16 since 1980. Since 1991 every ACC team has made at least one NCAA appearance, testament to top-to-bottom balance and competitiveness unrivaled in college basketball.

November 1984:

"It was easier to be a dominant team in the ACC in the '50s and early '60s because there were three teams that didn't really care about basketball since there wasn't any money involved. When I came with Frank (McGuire), he said he got six sure wins in the conference—two South Carolina, two Clemson, and two Virginia."

October 1977:

"I know one thing—whoever the sports writers pick to finish last, won't."

July 1984:

"We can be first to last, I mean it, and so can everybody else."

November 1984:

"There's balance because there are contests. (Nobody knows) for sure who'll win. A spread would be six to eight points every ballgame. That's two points for every 10 minutes played."

November 1984:

"We've gotten almost too much national publicity. The other leagues have a tendency to want to show, 'Hey, they're not that good.' And when we play against them, they're playing our league. That happened to Big Eight football some time ago when they were going strong. They all lost bowl games one year. They had five bowl teams and they all lost."

Smith celebrates his first ACC championship in 1969.

ACC TOURNAMENT

When the ACC was founded, only two other leagues held postseason championship tournaments. Critics said the ACC's decision to do likewise devalued the regular season, put too much pressure on a team to win three games for an NCAA bid, and drained the league champ on the eve of the NCAA Tournament. But by 1965 the ACC Tournament had become a perennial sellout and in 1975 the NCAA began allowing multiple entrants from the same league into its tournament, lessening the pressure to win the ACC championship.

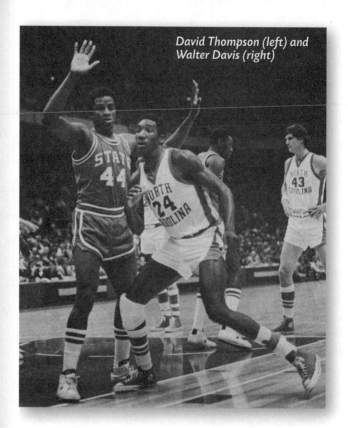

David Thompson (left) and
Walter Davis (right)

January 1988:

"In a way, the ACC Tournament makes sense now. In the old days it really didn't. To me, there was no way you could say that the best team was the one that won a three-day tournament instead of proving itself over an extended regular season. It would be analogous to having a one-set U.S. Open tennis tournament, or a one-game NBA playoff."

March 1992, citing Smith Barrier, sports editor of the *Greensboro News and Record*:

"The first time I got a team into the (NCAA) Tournament was 1967, and I was just relieved that it had finally happened. We were playing the ACC Tournament in Greensboro and we had to come from behind to beat N.C. State, and we had to come from behind to beat Wake Forest, and then we came from behind and beat

Duke. Smitty wrote a headline that said 'Duke To Win Tournament' and wrote about Duke—you know, Bob Verga and Mike Lewis and those guys. Larry Miller clipped the headline out of the paper. He didn't like it. And when the game against Duke had ended, he still had it. He'd carried it in his pocket. And he handed it to Smitty after the game."

March 1987:

"I'm probably more sensitive than the players (are) about our tournament performance the last few years...There are always reasons. But sometimes the excuse is that the other team played great."

March 1997, after defeating N.C. State, 64-54, to win the ACC title:

"It is special to be champion. That's the great thing about athletics—it says in black and white you won."

CHAMPIONSHIPS

Under Smith, North Carolina achieved a level of consistent excellence rarely matched in the history of American sports. The Tar Heels routinely won at least 20 games, reached the NCAAs, and finished among the top teams in the ACC. Yet, the coach was dogged by questions about his failure to win championships—the Tar Heels reached the Final Four in 1967, 1968, 1969, 1972, 1977, and 1981 without capturing a title. Critics said Smith's system prevented players from stepping out of the mold to rise to an occasion.

Autumn 1981:

"I don't like to talk about myself, but one of my coaches looked it up, that 30 coaches have won the national championship and only three coaches have been to the Final Four six times. Now, which do you think is a harder mountain to climb? The one 30 coaches climbed, or the one three did?"

" I'd like to win [the NCAA championship] just so people would stop asking me about it."

—*Autumn 1981*

February 1988, describing 1982 championship:
"We beat Georgetown that night by one point. That one point should not change the perception of me. It certainly doesn't determine how good or bad I am as a coach."

THE NCAA TOURNAMENT

Smith had a 65-27 record in NCAA competition, the most wins by any coach. His teams appeared in the tournament 27 times, including every year from 1975 through 1997. Smith's Tar Heels advanced at least as far as the Sweet 16 on 20 occasions, and to the Final Four 11 times.

December 1981:
"Everybody asks about (not winning) the NCAA (champhionship). It's just one of many goals. I'd like to see each team win it—not for me, but for them. I empathize with Jack Hartman at Kansas State. He's made the Final Eight several times when he had no business being there. Yet they ask him why he can't win regional championships."

November 1981:
"We've never had the best team. I think if I'd thought we'd had the best team it would bother me, but that hasn't happened."

January 1986:
"The first game of the NCAA Tournament is always a little bit shaky. I was for the 64 teams, because if you are one of the better teams you should get a team in the first round that you should beat. I would go a step further and

say the top 32 seeded teams should play the first game on their home court. There would still be upsets, but the regular season should mean something."

March 1989:

"It's the same every year. You've got to be healthy, number one. Number two, you have to be very, very good. Three, you have to be very lucky in hitting the right psychological situation.... You have to win a game when you don't play well to be successful in most tournaments. We're one of 60 teams that can go to the Final Four this year. You can be assured that the top four seeds this year won't be there. I don't think that's ever happened. That's the beauty of our game. In one game, anything can happen. That's what makes it so interesting. I don't think anyone is head and shoulders above the others.... We all gear our season to get to the NCAA Tournament."

June 1989:

"The NCAA Tournament now is not the fair method of determining the champion, but it's the most interesting one. One game, you're gone."

December 1992:

"We've become— which John Wooden predicted—like an Indiana high school tournament. Which is great for interest, I think. But your conference championship is cheapened. More teams would

Michael Jordan celebrates the 1982 National championship.

probably get to the Final Four—they're not necessarily going to win it—than win their conference tournament."

"*I don't think any of the lettermen can really express the family atmosphere that he's built, the tradition that he's built of loyalty and camaraderie. It's a fraternity that's very much admired by basketball people in the world. We get a lot of abuse because of our loyalty to one another, but we love being part of it.*"

—George Karl, head coach of the Milwaukee Bucks, before Smith's record-breaking 877th win on March 15, 1997

March 1988:
"I always like to play somebody in the NCAA Tournament that's already beaten us in the regular season."

March 1993:
"Momentum going into a tournament doesn't mean anything. It's trying to get your momentum within the tournament that does."

Only UCLA's John Wooden made more trips (12) to the Final Four than Smith (11). Wooden's visits came during a short span of time, while Smith's appearances covered four decades and a vast change in the status of the three-game event.

March 1991:

"Actually, playing your friends here is different than playing them in the regular season. You've already had great years. You won't feel very good if you lose, but still you'll be happy for the other one."

(KANSAS, COACHED BY FORMER SMITH ASSISTANT, ROY WILLIAMS, BEAT NORTH CAROLINA, 79-73, IN THE SEMIFINALS, THEN LOST TO DUKE IN THE TITLE MATCH.)

> *" Unfortunately the media makes more over 'Final Four' than they do 'Final Two', 'Final Eight'. It's easier to say, I guess."*
>
> —March 1993

March 1982:

"Some years I didn't think we'd make the Final Four, and we did. Some years we were knocked out in the first round when I thought we were the better team. Each time, I felt, 'Life goes on.'"

January 1995, on the 1977 Final Four; the Tar Heels hadn't been to the event since 1972:

"It became a circus at that time. I didn't believe it could be that big."

The 1982 national championship starting five (left: Worthy, Jordan, Perkins, Black, and Doherty)

THE 1982 NCAA CHAMPIONSHIP

For years, Dean Smith was criticized for creating a program that performed consistently well, yet failed to win championships. In 1968, 1977, and again in 1981, the Tar Heels reached the NCAA national championship game, only to fall short. Finally, in 1982, at the Superdome in New Orleans, North Carolina defeated Houston in the semifinals, then beat Georgetown, 63-62, on a jump shot by freshman Michael Jordan. North Carolina finished 32-2, playing essentially an iron-five: Jimmy Black, Matt Doherty, Michael Jordan, Sam Perkins, and James Worthy.

"I think I was out-coached tonight, but fortunately I had players that played extremely well.... I'm not sure we were the best team tonight—I think we were the lucky team."

HOME COURT ADVANTAGE

North Carolina has never had a losing home record in ACC competition. Until 1996, none of Smith's squads had lost more than two home conference games during a season. During Smith's 36 ACC seasons, his teams lost a mere 38 ACC home games, and lost consecutive home games just six times in 36 years—1965, 1973, 1981, 1985, 1990, and 1996.

June 1989:

"Our teams have done pretty well in road games, and that's been a proud achievement, because basketball is such a home court sport."

November 1975:

"We've lost some of the awe we once had at home. Teams used to come in here scared. I hope we can build some of that back."

June 1989:

"You're just a little quicker defensively or a little quicker (to the ball) at home. I know a pro team that actually would press all the time at home and wouldn't press on the road."

February 1985, referring to Carmichael Auditorium, precursor to the Smith Center:

"Norm (Sloan, the former N.C. State coach) says Dean turns the heat up in there. There are people who really believe I would tell some janitor, make sure it's hot in there. I tell you a sure way it's going to be hot—if it's hot outdoors and all of a sudden 10,000 people show up."

June 1989:

"I have a hunch that the home crowd does have an effect both ways.... When we're playing a team we should beat—it's usually somebody out of the conference— we're down, the fans look up and we're down 19-9, and they go, 'Ooohh.' It isn't out of support. It's a, 'Come on, you guys, you've got to get going' type of performance.... The noise makes some people lose their poise on the road."

INJURIES

Some of Smith's best teams were handicapped by injuries, notably a 1977 squad that still reached the NCAA title game and an '84 group that never recovered after Kenny Smith broke his wrist. Yet the Tar Heels haven't lost a major contributor to a season-ending injury since James Worthy broke his ankle in 1980.

December 1992:
"If you have to have them, have them in January, December, like we're having now. It gives other people time. But not in March."

March 1995, contemplating whether to allow injured Rasheed Wallace to play against Murray State in the opening round of the NCAA Tournament. (Wallace ultimately sat out the game.):
"I am a sucker for a poor, injured player."

March 1995 (Smith's 1977 team advanced to the NCAA title game despite big man Tommy LaGarde's broken leg, wing Walter Davis' broken finger, and Phil Ford's dislocated elbow.):
"I wouldn't suggest to anybody for motivational purposes to get three of your best players hurt."

OFFICIALS

Smith wasn't one to suffer officials lightly. He second-guessed them and acted out his favorite calls, such as arching his back and bumping his belly to indicate undercutting inside. Smith didn't curse, but he did yell at officials; other times he merely clapped his hands once to indicate his displeasure. He was especially concerned that the trend in officiating was toward allowing rougher play. He clearly preferred a finesse game, although his teams were notoriously physical on offense.

February 1977:
"I wouldn't want to officiate. So much is going on away from the two officials that we need three. The game is simply faster than it used to be."

"After 17 years of marriage, you'd think they would give us a divorce,"
Smith said of longtime official Lennie Wirtz.

45

December 1975:

"We were playing at Kentucky. The NCAA said the benches were supposed to be on the side of the court, but Coach Rupp didn't care, he put us on the ends. Time after time, the referee kept blocking my view. I couldn't see the scoreboard, so I asked the ref, a fellow named Jackson who owned a tobacco farm in Lexington, what the score was. He said, 'Coach, don't worry. We've got you by two.' He claimed later that he was talking about the scoring difference."

January 1986:

"Officials—and somehow the best officials—have said that they don't want to stop the flow of the game, that they won't call things that don't make a difference. But what has happened is that they are not calling things that do make a difference. For instance, if I throw the ball in to you in the post and the defensive man pushes you in the back, and you end up four feet farther from the basket, I think that's a disadvantage. But they don't want to stop play. Deep down, I think they will never be criticized on television replays if they don't blow the whistle."

October 1993:

"I don't think anybody calls anything at the end of the game. You've got to get murdered. They say let the players decide, and that makes no sense whatsoever. One player's getting an advantage over another player, and that's the reason you have officials. Why not let the players decide, just start out with the honor system?"

February 1997, on not calling enough fouls:

"I think everybody's so worried about the viewer. I'm worried about the players, and their game."

February 1997:

"I don't say it's the development of the game, it's development of how the game is officiated. And then that dictates (how the game is played). Although I won't teach the illegal screen because I'll be so mad when it's called. It will be called once a game. If you're fouled 10 times illegally, you might get nine baskets, but I'm scared to death that one time (it's called) would be a key time."

February 1995, after losing at Virginia 73-71, when a foul was called on Rasheed Wallace as he defended a drive by guard Harold Deane:

"I'm really disappointed that a foul was called with four seconds to go."

RECORDS

February 1989:

"I've had games where I don't think I really had the team ready to win, and yet they won and I got credit for a coaching victory. And there have been other games when I thought they were ready, and they lost. Those go on my record too. You see, records are not always accurate measures."

RIVALRY

January 1987:

"What happens is that you really would like to win the natural rivalry games. Phog Allen, my college coach, used to say you have to win in your backyard before you can feel real strong."

December 1980, following the 11th and final edition of the two-day, Big Four Tournament involving Duke, UNC, N.C. State, and Wake Forest:

"It's harder to play in the Big Four than it would be to play the No. 1 and No. 2 two teams in the country, DePaul and Kentucky, back to back. In the Big Four, you're playing rival schools. You know them, and they know you."

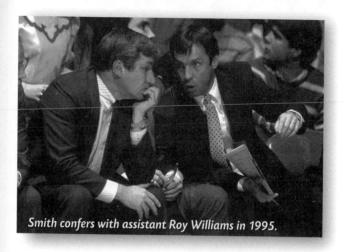

Smith confers with assistant Roy Williams in 1995.

Febuary 1987, on remaining a perennial favorite in the ACC:

"Over the summer, when coaches are watching tapes, they're watching Carolina tapes. That's the game they want to get ready for."

January 1991:

"It's hard for us to be the underdog. It's even hard for us to feel like we're the underdog, even when we should feel that way. And even more importantly, for the other team to feel like they're favored against us, that's hard to get across to them."

January 1996:

"It's the team that's the hardest to beat that is usually the biggest rival, and right now I'd say N.C. State is because that's our next game. I'll be saying that every game all year."

March 1984:

"I am amazed that there are people who think God, the Creator, wants one team to win an athletic contest. One pastor wrote to say that God answered his prayers when North Carolina won over Georgetown."

RULES

October 1993:

"So far, I think there hasn't been a major rule change that didn't work out for the best of the game, except when they said no dunking.... It was after '67 when (UCLA's Lew Alcindor) and (Houston's Elvin) Hayes were in the Final Four. Mr. (Henry) Iba was right in saying, 'In a way it makes them better players to shoot it.' But, then, there's the excitement of the dunk for somebody like me who's never done it. Kids were enjoying it. So that lasted until (Bill) Walton's years. Six years. It would be brought up every year. That's the only major rule change that lasted awhile that I don't think was better for the game."

October 1993:

"I think, finally, we're through with proposals to raise the baskets, which I've fought every year I can ever remember. When a coach says that—raise the baskets—it's to make the big guy a player. Of course it makes the big guy even more important because there's even more missed shots, and his size will help him rebound."

(PHOG ALLEN, SMITH'S COLLEGE COACH, WAS A LEADING PROPONENT OF RAISING THE BASKETS.)

STRATEGY

" I've always believed in quickness over strength or size."

—June, 1989

May 1992:

"We've always believed in the fast break. Ever since the first year I was head coach, you never saw North Carolina walk it up, (other than) in Four Corners late in the game...."

October 1995:

"I don't worry about the offense. We play together, we'll get shots. It may take us a while to get good shots."

Febuary 1975:

"I learned freelance play with Frank McGuire. I only used a patterned-type offense when we didn't have the big man.... Our offense is like UCLA's, but we have more freedom."

November 1983:

"I play the percentages and sometimes that might not be mentally good for the team. Who knows if we could have blown somebody out if we kept playing?... I've chosen long ago that if I'm going to coach and lose, I'm going to lose my way."

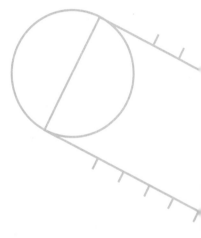

March 1981:

"You have a game plan, but it usually lasts for six minutes."

January 1964:

"Any time you lose I guess you can say you did the wrong thing."

STATISTICS

Few coaches relied more heavily upon statistical study than Smith. Both for purposes of measurement and control, he had student managers chart stats even during summer pickup games and pregame warm-ups. When the 3-pointer went into effect in 1986-87, he was among the first to study where rebounds went on missed attempts. He also developed his own statistical measures for points per possession, ball loss, rebounding, assists, and other aspects of the game. He tried to convince fans and the media to consider the importance of stats unrelated to scoring. And like most coaches, Smith was quick to dismiss the value of statistics whenever it suited him to do so.

June 1990:
"I only use statistics to reinforce what I already think, or if it's something unusual."

"People tend to look too much at numbers and not enough at where those numbers come from."
—Summer 1980

March 1994:
"Really, it's minutes played, not who starts."

February 1997:
"I don't go by rebounding margin. It has very little bearing.... To me, the key is the offensive rebounding."

June 1989, on how he records rebounds:
"We count if I keep it alive, that counts for us as an offensive rebound because it breaks down the defense. If I just tip it and I just keep it alive—I work hard and get a hand on it—then it breaks down their boxouts. If I get inside position and (the shot) is made, we get a half of an offensive rebound the way we keep it. 'If it comes off this side, it's all mine,'—and our teammate makes it, we want to give the guy some credit."

October 1993:
"The key statistic...
is still to get to
the foul line."

Smith discusses win No. 877.

SUCCESS

1977:

"Too often we think of basketball success in terms of points. That's why our players always point to the man who set up their basket. The fellow who rebounds and sets screens may go unnoticed, but he's just as important as the scorer. If I have a great one-on-one player who wants to do it all, I tell him, 'Fine, but I don't think I can come up with four players to put on the court with you.' He gets the idea."

WORDS FROM THE HUDDLE

Smith was noted for a reassuring calm in the huddle that infused players with confidence. Even at the most excited times, he was apt to remind his squads of the multitudes who didn't care about the outcome of the game. In keeping with Smith's exacting standards, huddles were arranged just-so, with players in the game, reserves, assistant coaches, and managers arrayed in prescribed places. Managers quickly swabbed perspiration from the chairs as soon as the players returned to the court.

January 1997:

"If we lose, we lose... It's not the end of the world.... There are a lot of Chinese who don't care. There are a few Carolina people who do care."

March 1982, to freshman guard Michael Jordan in the final seconds of the championship game against Georgetown, which was packed into a zone to prevent junior forward James Worthy from getting the ball (Jordan hit the winning jump shot.):

"Knock it down."

March 1993, after Brian Reese blew a dunk that would have won the game in regulation (UNC went on to defeat Cincinnati, 75-68, in the East Regional final.):

"All right. We haven't had overtime. We need the practice."

January 1993, down by 17 points with 9:21 to go (The Tar Heels rallied to defeat Florida State at the Smith Center, 82-77.):

"This is going to be fun."

" There were people calling (the day Smith retired) saying the news had brought them to tears. It's amazing. He's not curing cancer. He's not fixing the ozone hole. The reason why he's such a big thing is because he has so much class. He's humble to a fault."

— Matt Pencola,
Greensboro sports talk show host,
October 9, 1997

"James has a unique talent for a guy his size," Smith said of mobile, 6-9
James Worthy, a 1982 All-American and ultimately a seven-time All-Pro.

CHAPTER 2

People in the Game

" Coming out of high school, I had all the ability in the world, but I didn't know the game. Coach taught me the game—when to apply speed, how to use your quickness, when to use the first step or how to apply certain skills in certain situations. I gained all that knowledge so that when I got to the pros, it was just a matter of applying the information. Dean Smith gave me the knowledge to score 37 points a game, and that's something people don't understand."

—Michael Jordan,
Oct. 31, 1997

FRESHMEN

Smith treated freshmen differently from other players. They were assigned to carry tape or film equipment on the road. At practice they were the last to drink during water breaks and the first to chase loose balls. They were forbidden to speak with the media until they'd played a game. And freshmen typically struggled to master Smith's intricate system. Still, Smith took pains to point with pride to the number of freshmen who played significant roles and/or started in his program. Those who became starters as freshmen were Antawn Jamison and Vince Carter (1996), J.R. Reid (1987), Kenny Smith (1984), Brad Daugherty (1983), Michael Jordan (1982), Sam Perkins (1981), James Worthy (1980), Mike O'Koren (1978), and Phil Ford (1975).

Smith, with Antawn Jamison (left) and Shammond Williams, speaks with Andrea Joyce of CBS after win No. 877.

October 1983:

"There have been 11 basketball seasons since freshmen have been eligible for varsity play. At North Carolina, we have started freshmen on our basketball squad in eight of those seasons. I don't believe any nationally ranked basketball team has been helped more by freshmen eligibility than we have. Yet, even though 95 percent of our lettermen do graduate, there's no question in my mind they would have been better served educationally to have been ineligible for varsity play as freshmen. Almost all of the problems of intercollegiate athletics—excessive commercialism, compulsion to win, and the whole success/failure ethos—impinge directly upon the talented freshman student-athlete. If we are serious about wanting to minimize their adverse factors and place our primary concern on the student-athlete, we should eliminate freshman eligibility."

March 1989:
"The reason the vote was passed to play freshmen back in 1973 was to save money. Nobody will really say it's best for the student-athlete to play varsity as a freshman. They miss class. They miss their vacations. They have to spend more time in practice than they would if they were on an old freshman team."

October 1982:
"Freshmen should be ineligible, be academically oriented, have a year on campus before they're ready to play. Somebody says, if you feel that strongly about it, tell your freshmen they can't play. I say, I still like coaching."

CAMERON CRAZIES

Duke fans, dubbed the "Cameron Crazies," are notorious for their fervor, wit, and frequent slides into verbal abuse and rough mockery. Smith's teams were 18-18 at Cameron.

March 1996, after Duke students chanted "Asshole" at Jeff McInnis, UNC's abrasive junior guard:
"The coach is a role model and the players are—how about the students?"

FORREST "PHOG" ALLEN

Nicknamed "Phog" because he displayed a foghorn voice while umpiring a game in 1905, Forrest Allen coached in college for 48 years, the last 39 at the University of Kansas, where he reached the mandatory

state retirement age of 70 following the 1955-56 season. "Doc Allen," a practicing osteopath, often treated his own players and even major leaguers like Johnny Mize of the New York Yankees. His record was 746-264.

June 1988:
"Doc Allen was real strong on fundamentals. My gosh, we pivoted! We'd spend hours just pivoting."

December 1975:
"Our players signal me when they're tired, because Dr. Allen never thought you should get tired. He'd assume you were out of shape."

VINCE CARTER

Vince Carter, a tremendously athletic wing from Florida, played at North Carolina from 1996 to '98. Early in his career, he was considered soft and not particularly polished. By the time he was a junior he made second team All-America, and captivated audiences with his spectacular aerial feats. He departed for the pros after his junior season, following the advice of head coach Bill Guthridge and the retired Smith.

November 1996:
"He hasn't lost his jumping ability, but there's a lot more to the game than jumping."

BILLY CUNNINGHAM

Billy Cunningham, inherited from Frank McGuire's regime, played on the North Carolina varsity from 1963 to '65. Nicknamed "The Kangaroo Kid" for his jumping ability, he led the conference in rebounding and was first team All-ACC each year he played. The 1965 ACC player of the year, Cunningham went on to a successful career as a pro player and coach. He was inducted into the Naismith Basketball Hall of Fame in 1985 and voted to the NBA 50th Anniversary All-Time Team in 1996.

Vince Carter signals No. 1 from the bench during win No. 877.

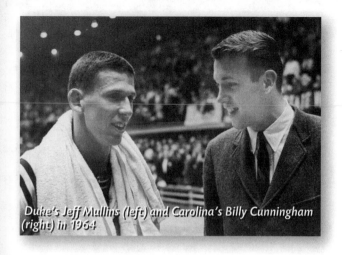

Duke's Jeff Mullins (left) and Carolina's Billy Cunningham (right) in 1964

January 1963, on a goaltending call during a loss to Wake Forest:

"I'm glad we have somebody who can jump that high this year."

December 1975:

"I did a poor job in 1964. Everyone was equal except Cunningham. We still didn't have any height, and I didn't really go with one lineup as I should have. Billy was criticized because it looked like he was loafing, but I asked him to do so much. If he got a rebound and we were fast-breaking, I told him just to stay at the other end of the floor."

HUBERT DAVIS

Hubert Davis, a 6-foot-4 guard, played at North Carolina from 1989-92. A modestly recruited player from nearby Virginia, among Davis' fondest early memories was a car ride back from the Montreal Olympics with his uncle, Walter Davis, and Phil Ford, then Davis' teammate. Davis was taken by Smith as much as a family favor as a serious prospect, and wound up among the best 3-point shooters the school has seen. As a senior in 1992 he made second team all-conference, and was a first-round NBA draft choice.

November 1988 (Davis played 248 minutes as a freshman, about seven minutes per game.):

"Hubert Davis is a little better than I thought he was, and I had him in camp for eight years... I knew he could shoot. We taught him to shoot. I knew he could pass.... I don't say this year, but he's going to play for us."

PHIL FORD

Phil Ford played at North Carolina from 1975 through 1978, and was arguably the best point guard in ACC history. Named 1978 national player of the year by several organizations, he was a three time All-American, and started for four straight seasons. Ford, quick and strongly built at 6-2, remains the leading scorer in UNC history (2,290 points). Many remember him best for the masterful way in which he directed Smith's "Four Corners" delay. Ford was NBA rookie of the year in 1979, and played seven pro seasons. He's been an assistant coach at North Carolina since 1989.

March 1982:

"As soon as we had a lead, I knew there wasn't any way we could lose. He was our Goose Gossage."
(GOSSAGE WAS ONE OF THE MOST INTIMIDATING—AND SUCCESSFUL—RELIEF PITCHERS IN BASEBALL AT THE TIME.)

"He saved my life. It was like, 'Hey, I'm here for you. You and I are going to solve this problem together.'"

—*Phil Ford, former UNC player and current assistant coach, on his successful battle with alcoholism*

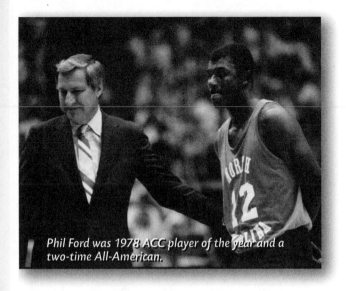

Phil Ford was 1978 ACC player of the year and a two-time All-American.

January 1986:

"Don't ever ask me to pick against Phil Ford. He's one of my all-time favorites."

1978, when asked what he'd do after Ford graduated:

"Resign."

RALPH SAMPSON

Ralph Sampson played at Virginia from 1980 to '83. The 7-foot-4 center, recruited avidly by North Carolina, was national player of the year as a sophomore, junior, and senior. The '80 team on which he played won the NIT title.

March 1989:

"We had some great battles with Virginia then. I never thought we'd beat them more than they beat us, but we did. Ralph's probably the only one I really missed on badly going into the pros. I thought he'd be a franchise. And he still may be. Sampson competed so hard. His teams won championships in high school. The three best years in Virginia's history were Sampson years."

RICK FOX

Rick Fox, a 6-foot-7 wing, played at North Carolina from 1988 to '91. A native of the Bahamas, he came to North Carolina by way of a high school in Indiana. Fox developed slowly, but was a first team All-ACC pick as a senior and a first-round NBA draft choice. He currently is a member of the Los Angeles Lakers, and an actor.

June 1989:
"He's had moments of being very, very good and moments of being very, very bad."

June 1989:
"Rick just can't help reaching. He has these tremendous hands—sure hands in addition to size of hands. That claw reaches out there and gets the ball a lot, but if the guy moves it, then he gets the arm."

Rick Fox in action

BILL GUTHRIDGE

Bill Guthridge, who once dated Smith's sister, served as an assistant to Kansas State coach Tex Winter for five years before coming to Chapel Hill for the 1968 season.

Coach Gutheridge and Coach Smith

Guthridge coached the UNC freshmen for six years, compiling a 75-25 record. He worked under Smith for 30 years before replacing him as head coach in October of 1997.

February 1996:
"Tex was always bragging on Bill, but what he didn't know was that I was taking notes. I knew Bill's family... My mother knew his grandfather."

August 1976:
"Bill Guthridge is the most organized person I've ever known. He was the one who was more the All-American boy in college."

October 1997, on Guthridge succeeding him:
"We have been together so long. We are straight with one another. I will be there anytime he wants to call, but I am not going to bother him. I don't want to be one of those coaches that hangs around."

ANTAWN JAMISON

Antawn Jamison, a 6-foot-9 forward, played his first two college seasons under Smith, and his final year for Bill Guthridge before going to the NBA. Remarkably gifted at grabbing offensive rebounds and quickly releasing shots,

Jamison made first-team All-ACC during each of his three seasons, and was national player of the year in 1998, the first Tar Heel to do so since Michel Jordan in 1984.

February 1996:

"He's not real strong in there, and I just get tired of seeing him start low, and the next thing you know he's pushed out. He's got to get stronger and hold his ground."

June 1996, following Jamison's freshman year:

"The second time through the league, they tried to get him off the boards at any cost."

June 1996, on why opponents gave Jamison open looks at the basket:

"Actually, they played everybody so they could shoot, except (Dante) Calabria. It's like the old story, 'Coach, I'm open, I'm open!' 'Son, there may be a reason that you're open.' "

March 1997:

"Antawn Jamison really has quickness, he has great work habits and exceptional hands, and he moves his feet well. At the next level of play he may learn to be a small forward, taking people off the dribble.... He has a huge heart, which is always important."

MICHAEL JORDAN

Michael Jordan played at North Carolina from 1982 through 1984. He was the ACC rookie of the year in '82, when the Tar Heels won the national championship. His jumper provided the winning margin, and gave his career a transforming boost of confidence. The 6-foot-4 guard—who later grew two inches—made first team All-ACC as a sophomore and junior, and was league and national player of the year in 1983-'84. Jordan left for the pros following his junior season, and was selected with the third pick in the NBA draft by Chicago. He has played for the Bulls ever since, and is widely regarded as the greatest player in the history of the game.

Jim Thacker of CBS interviews Michael Jordan.

March 1982:

"Michael didn't begin to bloom until his junior year in high school, and then he came on fast. But because he developed late, he still is working very hard to improve. He came in here with a great attitude. The toughest thing for a freshman often is to make the adjustment from being the star to being a part of a unit. Michael has done that very well."

December 1993:

"He didn't get recruited much until late in his senior year (in high school). His mother kind of liked Duke, because she liked Gene Banks. The only other school that seemed to interest him was UCLA, but they never offered him a scholarship."

Summer 1983:

"Michael listens. His first day of practice we noticed, here as a high school senior, he was trying to do what we said even though maybe it wasn't natural, say, from a defensive standpoint. But then, within three or four days he would have it down pat.... He continues to grow physically, and he has matured.... He was an outstanding prospect who has turned out better than we thought he would. He's better now, and he'll be even better next year because he is such a good worker, and he has ability. He has things to work on—his ball handling. That's this spring. Last summer I gave him a list of defensive principles to work on. This summer is more aimed at improving his outside shot.... As a freshman he was a better outside shooter than he was last year."

Summer 1983:

"He developed a high arc (to his shot) somewhere between the Georgetown game and our first practice, and we couldn't get over it. And he was making them, so we didn't want to say anything."

" *He's like a second father to me. When I first left school, I was unsure, nervous, scared going into a situation I wasn't really comfortable with and I didn't know if I was ready for it. He calmed me down.* "

—*Michael Jordan*

Summer 1983:

"Michael has been a small forward playing guard for us. But... he's been working on his dribbling and passing—he's going to be as good a prototype big guard that you could ever hope to find. In fact, we told him he can be a point guard in practice. Not that we're going to play him there, but that's how good we want him to become as a ball handler."

Summer 1983:

"He was so weak defensively as a freshman. He was trying to do all (the right) things, but they weren't habits yet. Last year they became habits to him, and now (he has reached) the next echelon.... He's free to go anywhere on the court in our defense. He can freelance because he's that sound."

(JORDAN MADE THE NBA'S ALL-DEFENSIVE TEAM IN 1997-98 FOR THE 10TH TIME, A RECORD.)

March 1989:

"His best game as a freshman was in the national finals—not just the points, but he graded out the best. He didn't play that well against Houston (in the semifinals). Then, all of a sudden in his sophomore season, I couldn't believe him in preseason practice. In every drill his team would win. He grew two inches and he improved his speed, quickness, and jumping ability through natural maturity."

October 1983:
"We worked really hard on that—growing."

Michael and his Mom

Summer 1983:
"He wants to do well, and he isn't ever satisfied, and that's true in his academic work. He was a very good student in high school, and here he's done well.... I give Michael some credit, but I give most to his family... it's a very close-knit, sound, high-type family."

Summer 1983:
"There is a quiet confidence about him. He doesn't jump out and say, 'I'm better than you.' "

" He listens, then goes out and does it. He's very coachable."
—October 1983

October 1986:
"We weren't even sure Michael Jordan would start until a week before (his freshman) season. That shows how smart we are."

January 1988:
"His charisma is something I can't believe.... It's just eerie."

January 1996:
"He's so excited about this year, almost like a rookie. He worked harder for this year, and I think it shows. "
(IN HIS FIRST FULL SEASON BACK IN THE NBA AFTER QUITTING IN THE WAKE OF HIS FATHER'S DEATH, JORDAN WON THE LEAGUE SCORING TITLE AND MOST VALUABLE PLAYER AWARD, AND LED CHICAGO TO THE NBA CHAMPIONSHIP.)

SAM PERKINS

Sam Perkins played at North Carolina from 1981 through 1984. He was ACC rookie of the year in 1980-'81, when the Tar Heels reached the national title game. He was a starter on the 1981-'82 championship squad. Perkins made first team All-ACC and All-America in each of his last three seasons. The 6-9 post player remained in the NBA through the 1998 season.

November 1981:

"He's probably, looking back, the first time we've had a true shotblocker. That gives you a dimension that just does wonders."

Sam Perkins does the honors after Carolina netted the '82 title.

CHRISTIAN LAETTNER

Christian Laettner played at Duke from 1989 through 1992, leading the Blue Devils to consecutive national titles in 1990-'91 and 1991-'92. The 6-foot-11 New Yorker made first team All-ACC as a junior and senior, and was the ACC and national player of the year in 1991-'92.

March 1992:

"I shouldn't say this, but I'd like to give him the Academy Award, too. He's the best actor since Meagher."

(DAN MEAGHER PLAYED FOR DUKE FROM 1982 TO '85.)

FRANK MCGUIRE

Frank McGuire coached in high school for 11 years, in college for 30 at St. John's, North Carolina, and South Carolina, and for a year (1961-'62) with Philadelphia in the NBA. He led St. John's to the Final Four in 1952, and North Carolina to the NCAA title in 1956-'57 with a 32-0 record. Noted for his ability to attract players from New York with his "Underground Railroad," McGuire was inducted into the Hall of Fame in 1976. He retired in 1980 with a career mark of 550-235. He died in October of 1994.

December 1975:

"Frank did things differently. I don't guess I'd met anyone like him before. He was loose and relaxed. He could get on his players without their taking offense."

March 1986:

"Frank wasn't into the technical aspects of coaching, but he was good at the politics that go into coaching. That is why I always dress with a tie. I learned that from Frank.... He was a master psychologist and motivator."

November 1992:

"He was a great leader. That's probably the best thing I

can say. I can say a lot of nice things, don't get me wrong, but (he was) an exceptional, charismatic leader."

November 1992:
"He always coached from a confidence standpoint, telling a player, 'What do you think I recruited you for?'"

November 1992:
"I don't think it's fair to say he wouldn't play them unless they were from New York. That's true, but it's a terrible thing to say."

October 1994, upon McGuire's death:
"I wouldn't be in North Carolina except for Frank McGuire asking me to come as his assistant."

KING RICE

King Rice, a 6-foot-1 point guard from upstate New York, played at North Carolina from 1988 to '91. Tough, and a solid passer and defender, he was a questionable outside shooter and an inveterate trash talker.

October 1989:
"He has got to remain healthy, like (President) Bush has got to remain healthy. Although I don't know who our Quayle is."

JERRY STACKHOUSE

Jerry Stackhouse, a highly recruited 6-foot-6 wing from North Carolina, played for the Tar Heels in 1994 and 1994-'95. "Stack" was an explosive, aggressive force at the offensive end. He's currently a member of the NBA's Detroit Pistons.

January 1995:
"I think Jerry is a natural leader, without doing a lot of talking. He's really a competitor inside, but you never know watching it from the outside."

Jerry Stackhouse, like most Tar Heels, elevated his game against Duke.

ADOLPH RUPP

Adolph Rupp attended the University of Kansas, graduating in 1923. Like Smith, he played under Phog Allen. He was head coach at Kentucky from 1931 through 1972 (the Wildcats didn't field a team in 1953 by NCAA edict). Rupp's teams won four NCAA titles (1948, 1949, 1951, and 1958), the 1946 NIT crown, 23 Southeastern Conference championships, and 876 games. He was elected to basketball's Hall of Fame in 1968.

1989:

"He didn't play (at Kansas). He was like sixth man on their great team, and he always held it against Doc Allen. I was sixth man, and I was thrilled I was that high."

November 1992:

"In a 40-point game, (Adolph Rupp would) get mad. Like, he beat this one team, it was 81-40, and he got mad at the sub—his name was Evans, I know him— because he'd let him in the game the last 30 seconds and his man scored. He wrote 81-38, 81-40. 'Now, what looks better in the paper?' Chewed that kid forever."

RASHEED WALLACE

Rasheed Wallace, a 6-foot-10 post player from Philadelphia, played at North Carolina in 1993-'94 and 1994-'95. As a sophomore he made first team All-ACC , led the league in field goal percentage (.654), and helped the Tar Heels reach the Final Four. An emotional performer, he left for the NBA following the 1994-'95 season and, like classmate Jerry Stackhouse, was an early first-round selection.

October 1995:

"He had more technicals than anybody else... Each time, my rule, he sits down next to me for five minutes. And he learned, because then the team has to run sprints for him the next time out."

BRAD DAUGHERTY

Often referred to by his coach as "Bradley," the 7-foot center played at North Carolina from 1983 through 1986. Erroneously reputed to be soft despite a martial arts background, Daugherty twice made all-conference and some All-American lists. His .620 career field goal percentage is among the best in ACC history. Daugherty, the first pick in the 1986 draft, went on to an all-pro career with the NBA's Cleveland Cavaliers, who retired his jersey in 1997.

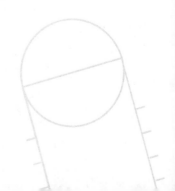

Brad Daugherty, 1983 in center

October 1987:

"Believe me, the first practices for freshmen are a shock. They've never been defended like that. I don't think Brad Daugherty can remember his first two months here. Sam Perkins just backed him in and scored every time. It's a big jump coming out of high school."

December 1987:

"If you told me when he first got here that Brad Daugherty would have been the first pick in the NBA draft, I would have laughed."

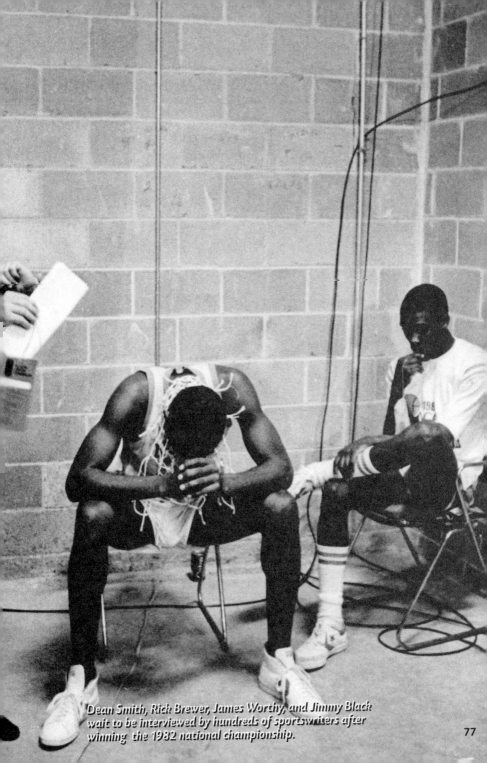

Dean Smith, Rick Brewer, James Worthy, and Jimmy Black wait to be interviewed by hundreds of sportswriters after winning the 1982 national championship.

Smith's Tar Heels routinely landed the best players in basketball-crazed
North Carolina, like Kinston's Jerry Stackhouse.

CHAPTER 3

On Teaching and Learning

"In order to stay on top, you've got to change, innovate, and develop, and he's done that. He was ahead of his time. He was far ahead of everyone else in the use of personnel. We have to change rules because of Dean."

—Norm Stewart,
Missouri coach

EDUCATION

Of 232 lettermen during Smith's 36 seasons at the University of North Carolina, 224 graduated—a success rate virtually unmatched at the major college level. The university achieved this high graduation rate despite admitting numerous academic exceptions. To help motivate his players to take their studies as seriously as they took basketball, Smith's assistant coaches followed younger players to class until they proved their trustworthiness as students.

May 1996, on using the NBA's advertising slogan to make a point about how many pros left college without degrees:

" 'You gotta love this game.' And, by the way, have a line underneath it: 'It's okay that not all of them graduate.' "

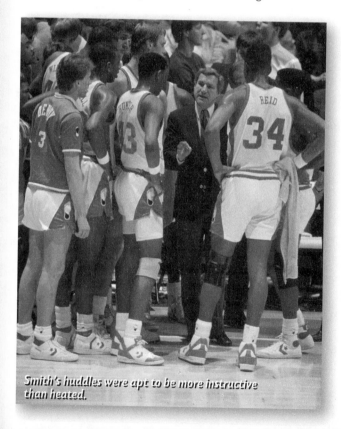

Smith's huddles were apt to be more instructive than heated.

October 1982:

"The university uses [athletes]. If we have a guy who plays four years and doesn't get his degree, we have used him. But if he plays four years and gets his degree, he has earned something in return."

October 1985:

"I believe the SAT examinations are culturally and economically biased, and they should never be used as a singular standard for admission. We have had an intelligent young man play for us who was between 600 and 700 on the SAT, who graduated easily. We also have had a player who scored over 1200 on his SAT, and who struggled to graduate."

May 1982:

"I really believe from now on I'm going to suggest to the pro team to have a figure for every course completed with a 'C' or better grade, you get a bonus. That way, you could say, 'This summer, I'll take three courses and make myself X number of dollars.'"

TEACHING

February 1996:

"Most teachers don't often have their students before that many people to see what they've learned... (There are) a couple of million assistant coaches watching the games, not (just) my own."

"Ninety percent of the stuff I learned, I learned from him. The other 10 percent I stole."

—Steve Reynolds,
former UNC manager,
on Dean Smith

March 1988, on ironing out team dynamics:

"That's why our practices are closed.... We're family, and it stays there."

> **" Remember, this is a dictatorship. I didn't say, 'Let's vote on this to see how much you should play.'"**
>
> —*March 1994*

October 1995:

"I'm talking about becoming a better player, doing well in school, getting their degree. Those are things that I hope (they want), and to enjoy the camaraderie of the team with a common goal."

October 1997, upon retiring:

"What I want to do is teach. If I were a doctor, I would go teach in the hospital. I want to tell the physical education people that I want to teach a course on basketball."

LEARNING

March 1983:

"We just repeat, repeat to build habits. You have to get that done, not wait until their junior year."

June 1988:

"To do something all the time, not some of the time, is essential to becoming a top basketball player."

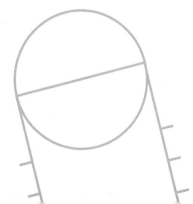

June 1992:

"How do you gain confidence? Through success."

Despite talented players like Kevin Madden, UNC missed the Final Four from 1983 through 1990, Smith's longest drought.

BEING A COACH

March 1982:

"I don't ever remember wanting to be anything but a coach."

October 1982:

"My dad was a high school football, basketball, and, in those days, baseball coach. Phog Allen begged me to go into medicine, but I've always wanted to coach because I could see Dad was very happy. The players were always coming around the house. When they came back from World War II, the first stop they'd make is our house."

March 1981:

"I was always interested in the Xs and Os, especially in football. I remember drawing up my first play, and my dad showing me why it wasn't good. It was a double wing play but I forgot to block somebody."

Autumn 1979:

"I wanted to be a football coach, but I'd have been fired long ago. On fourth down and inches in our own territory, I'm the kind that would try the bomb for the touchdown."

August 1980:

"The easiest way to coach is to do everything the crowd

wants you to do. Don't ripple the waves. But there again, you know the game better than the crowd knows it or you shouldn't be coaching."

October 1982:

"So help me, my first year in Chapel Hill, I got talked into coaching a Little League baseball team. What an experience! I was going to go out, put the value on participation. We were going to have a lot of fun. We were going to try hard to improve. We were going to play everybody equally and see what happens. And, my gosh, what happened? Parents were calling me names... they were living through their children."

March 1971:

"Some of the most successful coaches aren't ever over .500. It's what you do with what you've got that counts. The ideal situation for judging us all as coaches would be to eliminate recruiting. Have everybody get a team from their student body. Coaches remain constant. Players change."

" The coach gets too much attention, too much credit, and too much blame."

—*Summer 1980*

Summer 1980:

"Overcoaching is the worst thing you can do to a player. I think every coach knows that."

January 1997:

"(I'm) not as competitive as people describe me. You like to do well in your work and your job. I felt bad last year on a win more than on some losses, so it isn't determined by wins or losses. Is that competitive?"

December 1989, following a 19-point loss to DePaul:

"I've never been a patient man. I demand more of my players at this stage of the game than they're capable of giving."

November 1996:

"I should be more patient, you know, like a grandfather."

December 1972:

"I don't think coaches are in it for the money. I know I never was, and I didn't make much when I started. For me, it is the personal relationships. That's what I enjoy most, getting involved with your players."

"We've never had anybody better defensively for us," Smith said of point guard Derrick Phelps.

December 1993:

"Today, we rate all the high school kids so high, and then make them feel bad if they don't start right away or even if they have a good college career, because someone said they were supposed to be great. We talk about high school kids becoming pro players, that's just wrong. What I really like is finding a player who isn't highly recruited. I didn't even want to sign Hubert Davis, but he was Walter's nephew and he wanted to play for us so much. So we gave him a scholarship even though we weren't sure how good he was, and he became a first-round draft choice for the Knicks....That is the best part of coaching for me."

Smith confers with assistants Phil Ford (left) and Bill Gutheridge.

JUDGING COACHES

December 1981:
"There's too much talk about coach against coach. It's team against team, or institution against institution. I'm only 5-feet-10—all these other coaches can take me into the pivot."

March 1982:
"I don't think I'm a better coach now because we won a national championship. I'm the same coach."

October 1985:
"Good coaches who will not cheat, then do not win, will be fired, while coaches who cheat and win will be tolerated."

THE JOY OF COACHING

March 1971:

"You're in the ACC final, and the house is packed and the crowd is going wild, and the band is playing, and it's a minute before tipoff. You fall in love with that."

December 1976:

"I love the ritual. Recruiting in the spring, camps and clinics in the summer, practice in the fall and, in the winter, the easiest part—the games. I find each change of the seasons gives me a lift, rejuvenates me.... Whenever I look at a new group of freshmen coming to play basketball for the University of North Carolina, it makes me feel like I want to stay four more years."

January 1972:

"Each May I let out a huge never-again sigh after the season and the recruiting and speaking at 25 consecutive meetings of our Educational Foundation (the booster organization). But when October 15 draws closer, I start getting excited all over again."

October 1973:

"I wouldn't leave college coaching. I enjoy it too much. Why? It's a new team every year, new leaders, new faces. It's a challenge. I've often wondered about coaches who have quit. I wonder how they feel come October 15, when we open practice."

Smith with Duke coach Mike Krzyzewski

October 1982:

"When I chose to go into coaching at the college level, my chances of finishing as a college basketball coach were about one in a hundred. They'll all be fired somewhere along the line, or become athletic directors or writers or something like that."

March 1981:

"If I had known years ago that coaching would involve the travel, the interview time, and all the other things that go with it, I might not have become a coach."

March 1991 (The Tar Heels reached the Final Four.):

"I'm lucky. You probably have the same job, the same desk, each year. I have a different team each year. What a team this year!"

> *"Basketball-wise, he hit me with things defensively I had never heard before. I thought, 'No one has ever told me to do this, but it works.'"*
>
> —*Donnie Walsh,*
> *Indiana Pacers president*
> *and former UNC player,*
> *on Dean Smith*

November 1981:

"I have had the opportunity to coach and be general manager in the NBA, but I think I was meant for college basketball. I like the college atmosphere, visiting with professors. I like to see young men come along at this age, mature, and graduate. I don't like the big city."

December 1993, on coaching in the NBA:

"Why...coach where two guys play offense and the other three watch? That never appealed to me. That's terrible basketball."

Like UNC center Eric Montross, Smith wore "00" in junior high.

Larry Brown (left), Dean Smith, and Mildred the Bear on the golf course

CHAPTER 4

The Game of Life

"Loyalty is his defining grace. Dean probably knows the whereabouts of every player who ever played for him whether he was an All-American or a bench warmer."

—Paul Hardin,
former chancellor
at UNC, in 1987

BEER ADS

Smith—who is known to have a Scotch now and then, and who took pains to point out he wasn't moralizing about adults consuming alcoholic beverages—was alone among ACC coaches as he spoke against the hypocrisy of the conference's public posturing against drugs while it derived more than a half-million dollars per school in beer advertising revenue each year. Finally, at Smith's prompting, the University of North Carolina dropped all beer ads on its radio network and in its publications.

Smith stays on the ball in the 1997 NCAA Tournament.

October 1993:
"I'll have a beer. I'm not against it. But up to nine at night, it's the leading cause of teenage death. They say the ACC is fighting drugs, (yet) they're taking money from Budweiser."

March 1996:
"If aspirin were the leading cause of death for college-age students, Bayer would be off television."

CHEATING

Smith avoided even a hint of impropriety in recruiting. He was, however, an astute observer and critic of the college scene. Given his stature, he was heeded when he spoke against cheating .

Speech in Atlanta at Georgia High School Athletic Clinic:
"Society points the finger and says, 'You squealed.' At the same time society often overlooks the person who has done wrong. This doesn't make sense to me. I'm all in favor of doing more to police recruiting, including spending more money for NCAA investigators. And I see nothing wrong with coaches working within the system to deal with recruiting violations."

1980s:
"Ending freshman eligibility would also do away with schools getting a quick fix in recruiting. There was less cheating when freshmen were ineligible."

March 1982:
"It all goes back to a society problem, in that so many fans really don't care. They want their team to be No. 1. Our presidents of the universities have to come out and say, 'He's our coach whether he wins or loses—and he's gone if he cheats.'"

Speech in Atlanta at Georgia High School Athletic Clinic:

"Too many coaches have hurt their profession by saying, 'I won't cheat to win', and offering that merely as an excuse for losing. By making that statement a coach is implying a lot of others do, in fact, cheat. It is a convenient way of satisfying the alumni in a losing situation."

CORRUPTION

Smith has said he'd like to teach a course on society and sports now that he's retired. The manner in which American values have corrupted intercollegiate sports is one of his favorite topics.

October 1982:

"As soon as we have revenue sports and there's more money, then we have more problems."

October 1982:

"If somebody has a lot of money, it's amazing how the universities go bowing down to them, even though they may have gotten the money the wrong way.... They cheated. They've stolen. And all of a sudden they have a lot of money—and then the universities go bow to them."

> *"It's an incredible thing. It's like Cy Young's record 511 wins. A 20-game winner for 25 years and you still can't beat the guy."*
>
> —*Princeton coach Bill Carmody, March 15, 1997, after Smith's 877th victory*

*" My college coach,
Phog Allen, once told me,
'Dean, you can't stop at
every dog that barks
or you'll never get the
mail delivered.' "*

—*Autumn 1978*

July 1982:

"I honestly mean it when I say I don't think I'm a better coach because Jordan's shot went in, but 'they,' the people out there, say I am. A buddy of mine said he laughed when he thought about the fact that our teams had done so well that I had probably the best situation of any coach, but people were feeling sorry for me because we hadn't won the NCAA championship.... This team did me a big favor by getting the monkey off my back. I didn't think I had one but I kept reading it."

December 1977:

"My players and assistant coaches and close personal friends are the only ones who I care what they think about me."

October 1982:

"People used to think I made it up, but I didn't feel like we had to win a national championship to feel like we were doing a good job coaching. But other people say that. Well, I don't live by what other people say. I admit, It still bothers me. I'm human, and it bothers me when everybody's on me."

June 1988:

"Unfair criticism probably doesn't bother me. If it's fair it probably bothers me."

June 1989, reflecting on his fourth season, when he was hanged in effigy on campus:

"My first two years, it was all gravy. Everybody was patting me on the back. We weren't supposed to win any games. We lost all our players to the NCAA probation. I deserved it (criticism) in '64 but they didn't give it to me until '65."

February 1989:

"I'm kind of excited. This year I'm getting letters. Of course they're not signed..."

DISCIPLINE

Discipline was a prominent feature of Smith's North Carolina program, from the way in which players were to comport themselves on the floor to the way they dressed on the road and behaved in class. Discipline was imposed in a variety of ways, from peer pressure to direct coaching intervention.

"The really free person in society is the one who is disciplined."

—October 1982

July 1984:

"Players haven't changed. They still want to be disciplined.... They feel loved when they're disciplined."

June 1985:

"I believe that the disciplined guy can do anything. He can choose to stay up late, he can choose to smoke 10 packs of cigarettes. He chooses.... Usually the people coming into the ACC have had to have some discipline or they wouldn't be that good. They've had to say no a lot of times to other things to go work on their basketball."

1988:

"If a rule is broken, we punish as a team. We believe in group punishment for an individual infraction. We have found this peer-pressure method far more effective in building team morale than motivation created by fear, reward, or any other means."

June 1996:

"Interesting, when Larry Brown came back as my assistant, he said, 'Coach, you're not as hard on these guys as you were on us.' When Eddie Folger came back as my assistant, he said the same thing. Dave Hanners and Phil Ford say the same. Whether that's their perception or whether it's true, I don't know. I think I've always dealt with the individual."

Mitch Kupchak (GM of the Lakers) and Bobby Jones (NBA great) in stands during No. 877. Coach Smith was touched that his past players were at Winston-Salem.

HISTORY

Smith is quite aware of the contributions of his predecessors in the coaching ranks, and readily credits those from whom he learned. But, not one for public self-congratulation, he's loathe to discuss his place in the game's pantheon.

October 1997, when asked about his place in history on the occasion of his retirement:
"There is no such thing as the greatest ever. We all try to do our jobs to the best of our abilities."

October 1997, on how he'd be remembered as a coach:
"I don't know, nor have I given it any thought... He knew a little basketball, and he did a good job and then lived happily ever after, and loved his players and received loyalty in return."

IMAGE

Smith's image—and a perceived gap between how he wanted to appear and who he was—remained a subject of heated debate for much of his career, particularly during the 1970s. He preferred to be seen as a sportsman, educator, and reformer, and did what he could to control countervailing information, as when he smoked cigarettes behind the bleachers or otherwise out of sight. "He has more technical fouls than anyone in the ACC, and yet he's pictured as the greatest gentleman," said Terry Holland in a 1977 conversation with Richmond reporter Jerry Lindquist that the Virginia coach claimed was off-the-record. "He works very hard at building the proper image."

November 1981:
"What image?"

1981:

"Is it image if I yell at my players in practice but don't during a ballgame because I don't want to embarrass them? Is it image if I say nice things about the other team? I say what I believe, just not everything I believe."

March 1981:

"I certainly won't criticize one of my own players. They work too hard to have me knock them in public. If I have something to say to them, I do it alone. The problem is, whenever I say something nice about somebody we've beaten everybody says, 'Dean's doing it again.' I'm not. I mean everything I say. It's just that I don't say everything I'm thinking."

INTEGRATION

Long before racial reconciliation became a common goal—particularly in the segregated South—Dean Smith helped break a color barrier by accompanying his pastor, Robert Seymour, and a black theology student to a restaurant in Chapel Hill. Smith began recruiting black players as soon as he became head coach. He courted Greensboro's Lou Hudson, and later signed Elm City's Willie Cooper, who quit basketball to concentrate on his studies following his freshman season in 1965. Smith's first African-American player was Charlie Scott, a member of the varsity

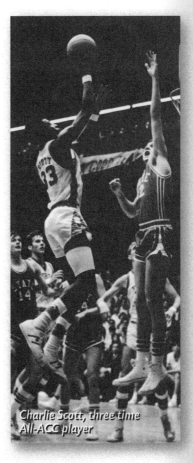

Charlie Scott, three time All-ACC player

from 1968 to '70. (Scott wasn't the first black player in the ACC. Maryland's Billy Jones was, debuting during the 1966 season, when Cooper would have joined the UNC varsity.)

"He coached for all the right reasons—and the first reason was always the players."

—John Swofford,
   ACC commissioner and former athletic director at UNC,
   upon Smith's retirement

February 1987, on Chapel Hill in the late 1950s and early 1960s:

"They called it the liberal voice of the South. We just had to get it to basketball."

April 1987:

"Basketball has done a lot for racial justice."

January 1991:

"Go through civil rights again? Yeah, I'll be there."

LOSING

Over the course of Smith's 36 seasons the Tar Heels averaged just seven losses per year.

February 1975, contemplating a 65-62 loss at Virginia:

"I haven't seen the time I couldn't get upset after a loss. I'm trying to work on my maturity, though. I do know that it's not all life. I'm trying to get things on more of an even keel. I'm not as elated with victory as I once was, because there's always another game."

November 1996:
"Maybe it would be good to be blown out early, and wake up."

February 1988, after losing at home to Temple:
"I might start drinking now."

March 1989, after losing at home to Duke:
"I have some work to do on myself. I'll see my wife tonight. She's a psychiatrist."

January 1997, with the team's record at 9-4:
"I admit, if we lose a few more I'll settle for playing poorly, and winning."

MILESTONES

Smith resolutely refused to concede the importance of his achievements, or to take pleasure in the milestones that measured them. In fact, as in many other areas he was remarkably consistent in his dismissive responses across the years.

From left: Sam Perkins, Michael Jordan, Lennie Rosenbluth, Mike O'Koren, and James Worthy, five of UNC's all-time stars at an Alumni game to open the Dean Smith Center in Chapel Hill

January 1976:

"I'm not one to live in the past or to live on records. The only things I look back on are the players who have graduated, how well they've done after leaving school."

February 1, 1980, after his 400th career win:

"I have 200 more wins than Bear Bryant. A baseball coach could get 400 wins in 10 years. It just mean's I'm getting old. It's just longevity."

(BRYANT COACHED FOOTBALL AT ALABAMA.)

December 3, 1983, after his 500th career win:

"That just means a long time coaching. I don't set any personal goals in coaching. I set team goals. It's just a nice win."

December 1983:

"It's just like golf. I've never lost to (Tom) Watson, but then I've never played him either. A lot of coaches haven't coached long enough to win 500."

February 11, 1987, after his 600th career win:

"This one was a little harder than the first one."

January 1991, on the eve of his 700th career victory:

"I really have trouble with all this. That kind of thing is for sports information directors."

January 9, 1991, after his 700th career win:

"It's nice for people who notice that, and I thank the players who have been here, but I was probably more excited after our team beat Virginia in that first game... I really don't like this business of counting coaches' victories. How can you say the coach won the game, anyway? It was all the players I've had the privilege to coach who won the games."

March 1992, on passing UCLA coach John Wooden for the most wins in NCAA Tournament history:

"If you look at that, you've got to put the all-time, double asterisk or something. Coach Wooden did that when you had to win your league. It's just a different ballgame."

December 1992, after tying Phog Allen for fourth place all-time among major college coaches (746 victories):

"I don't deal with that. I never have gotten into coaches' numbers. I'm interested in each team's numbers. I'm interested in those six wins. That's six wins closer to the NCAA tournament."

January 1990:

"A couple of sportswriters said, 'Hey, you can beat Rupp's record (876 wins).' First of all, I'm not sure I could. But that's something I would never want. And I'll guarantee you it'll never happen."

March 15, 1997, after surpassing Adolph Rupp's record with 877 wins:

"It's never been a goal of mine. It wasn't a goal at any point. I'm not that type of goal-oriented person. We've won 26 games. I want us to win 27. That's my goal."

March 1997, on whether the Rupp record was a distraction:

"Your question is a distraction."

RECUITING

Smith wasn't rated among the college game's best recruiters. Yet his teams regularly boasted many talented players, gathered without any hint of improprieties. The success of Tar Heel players in the NBA became a selling point, particularly among big men. Over the years, players around the country grew up watching— and rooting for—UNC.

August 1980:

"First of all we look to see who's a great player, and then we start to check his academic work to see whether he can graduate here or get into school. After that, we hope their teammates respect them in high school, and that's hard to do when they're the star."

November 1981:

"It's a shame our society has gotten to the point where they say how can you do it by doing it the right way? As if, you have to do it the wrong way. We're soft-sell recruiters, and our players do it for us."

January 1984:

"We ask them, 'What is your goal in college?' If their goal is to get an education and become a better player, we feel we have a good chance. If they want to average 30 points as a freshman, we don't."

November 1989:

"I'm not a good recruiter. I've never been one to talk a guy into signing. I don't want to talk him into signing. I want a player to select us."

October 1993:

"Recruiting is easier if you're winning, because you're going to be on television."

October 1993:

"Who's to say which guys are the best recruits?...
Somebody can be a much better college player and
yet won't be a pro. Some
guys are more suited
for college."

SATISFACTION

Summer 1980:

"There's lots of excitement
winning a game, a champi-
onship. People jump up and
down and hug each other. A
group gets together and gets so
determined in a single goal, and
achieves that goal. There is excitement in that, and something they look
back on and say, 'That was a great
moment.'"

March 1982:

"I enjoy succeeding and winning, but I
take the greatest pride in knowing
I did a good job."

March 1986:

"I don't think there is any one singular
thing you can say brings happiness.
We're very happy to have won as
many championships and as many
games. We have done it within the
rules, we don't cheat with recruiting.
I never had goals to win so many
championships or anything like that.
I try to get the best out of each team,
and for them to improve as players
and be a credit to the university. When
they do that I feel we have accomplished our goal."

At the NCAA in '97

October 1985:

"I think we are the only school that will applaud the visiting team at introductions. Our fans also refrain from waving their arms behind the backboard during an opponent's foul shot. We also were the first predominantly white university to actively recruit and subsequently sign black athletes south of Washington, D.C. Charles Scott and Willie Cooper led the way for so many athletes in the ACC, the Southeastern Conference, and the Southwest Conference."

October 1997, asked upon his retirement the achievements of which he was most proud:

"I would think it was the players who graduated here and went on and had very happy lives. They stay in touch, and they have enjoyed their experiences in Chapel Hill. I can't find one who has come to Chapel Hill, even those that transferred have come back and worked here in the summer camps. I haven't found any of them that think they made a mistake in coming here. I guess I would be most happy about that... It was a treat for other coaches to come in and say they ran our stuff and liked it. That's been special. The number-one thing has been the relationships with our players."

TELEVISION

January 1989:

"Television runs the game, in case you didn't know."

October 1985:

"Our coaches wanted to win as much before we were on television. Television has brought about more interest and a power to change the schedule, but not more desire to play well and win."

March 1992:
"The other day, I was watching something live and I started fast-forwarding. You think I watch too much tape?"

SOCIETY

February 1975:
"Politics, to me, should mean human rights."

February 1989, on talk he should run against Republican Senator Jesse Helms:
"I'd never get elected if people in North Carolina realized how liberal I am."

January 1991, during the Gulf War:
"Why can't the United States band together for some other good thing like (fighting) poverty? If you want to kill somebody, then everybody's for it."

April 1985:
"I'd just like to say that we really do need some new standards by which to measure success in our society. Genuine success is not going to the top, and staying there. I know a lot of people there who aren't very happy. Happiness is a by-product. If you lose yourself, then you're not happy. To be a success, there are three things you need to do: If you can do what you can, with what you have, where you are, then you can't be a failure."

SPORTSMANSHIP

October 1982:
"Notice how our guys don't get technical fouls. It is I that act foolish sometimes, and if it's necessary I'm going to be the one to look bad, not them. Because too many young kids are looking up to them."
(THIS STANDARD CHANGED IN SMITH'S LATER YEARS.)

CHAPTER 5

Dean Himself

"There is nobody like you—not just because you won, but because of the way you did it."

—President Clinton,
to Smith upon his retirement,
October 9, 1997

Designer Alexander Julian said Smith's 1990 request to redesign UNC uniforms was "like having God ask you to redo the uniforms for the archangels."

DEAN HIMSELF

Dean Smith isn't given to public introspection or display. For nearly two decades he's shunned personal interviews, lest they distract from the players and program at North Carolina. But over the years, in drips and drabs, we reveal ourselves in conversation, if only to make a point.

March 1981:

"I don't consider myself that much of a private person. I don't like it, though, when I'm cast as some kind of an expert on subjects that I'm not expert on. I'm just another human being with beliefs. People might listen to me because I'm a coach and I don't think that's right....
If I ever really started talking about Jerry Falwell and the Moral Majority, I'd be swamped with letters because I really have difficulty dealing with them. They upset me."

Smith remained outwardly calm in most circumstances.

June 1990:
"I can't be that smart. I am very careful."

June 1991:
"I'm not as manipulative as people think."

"I'm extremely organized in practice, but that's probably the only place."
—March 1997

February 1990:
"I still feel better if we play poorly and win, than I do if we play well and lose. I probably won't be able to change that. I said I'd change that before too long, but I still have difficulty, which means I care what people think."

November 1983:
"I'm a coach that second-guesses myself a lot."

January 1971:
"Win or lose, it's the same. I sleep the same, which is to say, very little. I do some of my best thinking between midnight and 2 a.m."

HIS CHILDHOOD

Smith grew up in a little stucco house in Emporia, Kansas. His father, Alfred, coached basketball, football, track, and baseball at Emporia High and his mother, Vesta, was superintendent of schools as well as a teacher in both high school and college.

March 1981:
"I was always taught as a boy that you don't brag about yourself."

Smith's parents, Vesta and Alfred, enjoy one of their son's victories in the Dean Smith Center.

January 1992:

"I was a pretty cocky ninth-grader. My dad was the coach and I was a kid who was always around the gym or the football field."

Autumn 1980:

"I was a quarterback in football. In those days, quarterbacks got to call our own plays and that was fun. I was a guard in basketball, which meant I got to call the plays. I was a catcher in baseball which meant I was in the game calling the pitches."

February 1987, on Alfred Smith's 1934 Emporia High squad, which won the state basketball title with black players, a first in Kansas:

"My dad was kicked out of the Kansas coaches' association for playing black players in 1935."

January 1992:

"We were taught to believe in the human family from day one.... Our team made a trip one time and we stopped at the Jayhawk Hotel to have a meal and they wouldn't serve Chuck Taylor. So dad and the rest of the team stomped out and went somewhere else to eat."

SMOKING

Smith started smoking cigarettes after college, and remained a chainsmoker for 30 years. He quit permanently on October 15, 1988, the start of practice for the 1989 season. Tobacco and strong drink were forbidden in Vesta and Alfred Smith's household.

January 1992:

"In fact, that's probably why I smoked for so many years. Just a form of rebellion."

March 1989:

"Yeah, I've heard about that: I've quit smoking so I won't get cancer, but I'll have a heart attack because I'm screaming at everybody."

HIS COACHING DEBUT

Smith followed the successful, charismatic Frank McGuire as head coach at North Carolina. McGuire, who left with NCAA and university-system penalties engulfing the program, recommended Smith, a defensive specialist, as his successor. The new coach turned 31 in 1962, near the end of his first season running the show. Smith's debut season ended with the only losing mark of his career.

June 1990:

"As I recall, [UNC Chancellor William Aycock's] words to me when he gave me the job were, 'Don't embarrass the university.' He didn't want any problems. He wanted good students, and he wanted no fights on the court and no NCAA problems. He said, 'Do it legally, and don't worry about winning.'"

March 1994:

"My first team didn't have anybody that could dunk the ball.... We were a great defensive team."

June 1990:

"When we went 8-9 that first year, people here were ecstatic."

January 1993:

"My first team may have played harder than any team we have ever had."

June 1990:

"I don't think I ever doubted my ability to coach, and maybe I should have."

"Dean Smith is more organized than crime."

— *Geno Auriemma,*
Connecticut women's
basketball coach, March 1995

DEMANDS AND DISTRACTIONS

Early in his career, Smith decided how he would handle the outside demands of his job—reticently. He created a series of obstacles through which interviewers, charity suitors, and others had to pass in order to gain a return phone call or a personal meeting. He kept to these self-designed rules throughout his years in coaching, and to a remarkable degree was able to maintain his emotional equilibrium.

January 1995:

"There's pressure in every job. A mother with three young kids really knows what pressure is."

October 1982:

"I've been careful to avoid overcommitting myself ever since 1972. We played in the Final Four that year, and the postseason commitments disrupted some priorities."

July 1982:
"I just leave some things undone. It's the only way."

December 1985:
"Things have changed a lot—TV has done that. I finally quit worrying about pleasing everyone. My time commitment has to be to the players, the school and my own staff... *Sports Illustrated* did a big story (about me), and I never even talked to them."

November 1993, on the inconvenience of meeting demands after winning an NCAA title:
"Really, my golf game suffered terribly, but I'm willing to let it suffer next summer."

Smith kept a firm grip, though he allowed players more on-court self-expression in later years.

November 1993:
"You don't know how long it takes to say no to everything."

January 1995:
"You set your priorities, and go from there."

BEING HANGED IN EFFIGY

Smith twice was hanged in effigy on campus during the 1965 season, his fourth. The first incident followed North Carolina's fourth straight loss, 107-85, against Wake Forest in Winston-Salem. Disgruntled UNC students hanged the coach in effigy in front of Woollen Gym. The Tar Heels won their next game, at sixth-ranked Duke, but following a home loss to North Carolina State, Smith's effigy was again strung up while a student played taps.

March 1981:
"You don't forget a thing like that, ever."

January 1990:
"I'm just glad they settled for hanging a dummy and not the real thing."

DIVORCE AND FATHERHOOD

Smith has five children—two daughters and a son from his first marriage, and two daughters from his second. He divorced his first wife, Anne, in 1973, and met his current wife, Linnea, on an airplane in 1976—she was reading "The Gospel According to Peanuts."

January 1986:
"I'm probably a better father now. The first time, I was probably coaching too much."

Smith and his most famous pupil, Michael Jordan, share a love of golf, the more competitive the better.

GOLF

Golf is Smith's passion. He was a golf coach at the Air Force Academy and remains a formidable and avid player.

1974:
"It keeps me mentally healthy.... With non-basketball people I can play golf and forget about things that happen in my everyday world."

March 1995:
"I'm never afraid. I'm not even afraid of a ten-foot putt. Not even downhill. If you miss, you miss. It goes on by."

October 1992, on an NCAA edict delaying the start of preseason practice:
"It helps my golf game. I am checking out a new course tomorrow."

117

SMITH CENTER

The Dean E. Smith Student Activities Center, located in a hollow near the edge of campus in Chapel Hill, is perhaps the largest and most expensive public building dedicated to a private, living American citizen. The Smith Center hosted its first event on January 18, 1986, when North Carolina beat top-ranked Duke, 95-92. The domed structure holds 21,572 for basketball and cost $33.8 million, funded entirely with private contributions from 2,362 donors.

January 1987:
"You've got to wonder about the priorities of a society that allows a basketball coach to work in a place like that."

January 1986, prior to the opening of the arena:
"That's never been a goal of mine, or one that would have any significance, to have a building or a road or a bathroom named after me."

June 1989:
"The way they said it—you're representing all the players—I couldn't say no."

January 1986, on the Dean Dome, the building's popular nickname:
"That's worse. It sounds like I don't have any hair."

INTERVIEWS

Smith wasn't one to suffer interviews lightly. In fact, he often turned them into mental arm-wrestling sessions. He looked repeatedly at his watch and was apt to remind reporters that he knew where they'd gone to school, as if that revealed their prejudices. He routinely deflected questions about himself, and warned his players to adopt his attitude of constant wariness.

Summer 1980:
"Too much is written about me. Write about the players."

July 1982, on refusing to cooperate with a *Sports Illustrated* profile by Frank Deford:
"I don't need it for my ego. We don't need any more ink in our recruiting because we've had plenty. It wouldn't be of any great benefit to anyone."

Winter 1986:
"You misquoted me. You wrote, 'If I was.' I'd never say that. I said, 'If I were.' That's proper grammar."

Unknown date, on Smith's post-game instruction to his players regarding comments to the media:
"Remember, brag on the other team and don't say anything about the officials."

RETIREMENT ANNOUNCEMENT

"I don't blueprint the future."
—*October 1997*

Dean Smith at his retirement press conference in 1997

*Coach Smith at the
1995 ACC Tournament*

THE NUMBERS

- 27 straight 20-win seasons

- 27 NCAA Tournament appearances (23 consecutive)

- 2 NCAA titles

- 11 NCAA regional Titles

- 17 ACC regular-season championships

- 33 straight ACC top-three finishes

- 4 NIT Appearances

- 1 NIT title

- 97 percent of players graduated

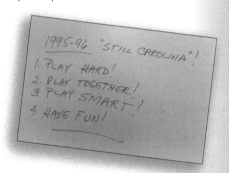

"Again, statistics don't tell the truth."

—August 1991

THE EARLY YEARS

- **Feb. 28, 1931:** Dean Smith born (Emporia, Kansas).

- **1949:** Smith graduates from Topeka High School with academic scholarship to University of Kansas.

- **1952:** Kansas basketball team, with Smith as a reserve guard wins national championship.

- **1955-58:** Smith is hired as assistant coach to Bob Spear at the Air Force Academy.

- **1958:** Smith is hired as assistant coach to Frank McGuire at North Carolina.

- **1961:** Smith, 30, replaces Frank McGuire.

1962
8-9 overall, 7-7 ACC regular season, tied for fourth.
Highlights: Smith was so nervous for his debut, an 80-46 defeat of Virginia, that he forgot to set aside a game ball. Only losing season of his career.

1963
15-6, 10-4 ACC, third.
Highlights: Upset Kentucky at Lexington, 68-66. With Larry Brown at the point, Smith developed the noted and much-derided "Four Corners" delay offense.

1964
12-12, 6-8 ACC, fifth.
Highlights: Most losses under Smith until 1990.

1965
15-9, 10-4 ACC, tied for second.
Highlights: Smith twice hanged in effigy on campus. Team followed first incident by beating sixth-ranked Duke at Durham, 65-62, and finished regular season with seven straight wins.

1966
16-11, 8-6 ACC, tied for third.
Highlights: Opened 8,800-seat Carmichael Auditorium with an 82-68 win over William and Mary. Tar Heels had a 169-20 record (an .894 winning percentage) in "Blue Heaven" over 22 seasons, all under Smith.

1967
26-6, 12-2 ACC, first; won ACC Tournament.
Postseason: NCAA Final Four; losses to Dayton and Houston.
Highlights: UNC won first ACC title since 1957. Reached Final Four for first time under Smith.

1968
28-4, 12-2 ACC, first; won ACC Tournament.
Postseason: NCAA Final Four; lost to UCLA in title game, 78-55.
Highlights: Twenty-game win streak during regular season. First back-to-back Final Four appearances by ACC program.

1969

27-5, 12-2 ACC, first; won ACC Tournament.

Postseason: NCAA Final Four; lost to Purdue and Drake.

Highlights: Won 18 of first 19. Only school in ACC history other than N.C. State (1954-56) to win three straight ACC championships. First ACC team to make three straight trips to Final Four. (Duke later went five straight times: 1988 to 1992.)

1970

18-9, 9-5 ACC, tied for second.

Postseason: NIT; lost in first round, 95-90 to Manhattan.

Highlights: Last time UNC failed to win at least 21 games under Smith.

1971

26-6, 11-3 ACC, first; lost in ACC Tournament final.

Postseason: Won NIT, defeating Georgia Tech in final, 84-66.

Highlights: First ACC team to win NIT, first title for Smith. End of streak of seven straight seasons with All-American on roster.

1972

26-5, 9-3 ACC, first; won ACC Tournament.

Postseason: Final Four; lost to Florida State, 79-75, beat Louisville.

Highlights: Fourth appearance in Final Four in six years. Ranked second in final AP and UPI polls.

1973

25-8, 8-4 ACC, second.

Postseason: NIT; 3-1 record with loss in semifinals, 78-71 to Notre Dame.

Highlights: Lost to N.C. State in final home game, last defeat in home finale until 1989.

1974

22-6, 9-3 ACC, tied for second.

Postseason: NIT; lost in first round, 82-71 to Purdue.

Highlights: Started four eventual pros. Overcame an 8-point deficit in final 17 seconds against Duke, winning 96-92 in overtime at Carmichael.

1975

23-8, 8-4 in ACC, tied for second; won ACC Tournament.

Postseason: NCAA; lost in East Regional semifinal, 78-76 to Syracuse.

Highlights: Defeated N.C. State's David Thompson in his last ACC contest, ending a nine-game Wolfpack win streak against UNC.

1976

25-4, 11-1 in ACC, first; lost in ACC Tournament final.

Postseason: NCAA, lost in first round, 79-64 to Alabama.

Highlights: UNC's Walter Davis, Phil Ford, Mitch Kupchak, and Tom LaGarde among seven ACC players on gold-medal winning U.S. Olympic team coached by Smith, assisted by Bill Guthridge and Georgetown's John Thompson.

1977
28-5, 9-3 in ACC, first; won ACC Tournament.
Postseason: NCAA; lost in national championship game, 67-59 to Marquette.
Highlights: Lost late lead to Marquette after much-criticized decision to go to Four Corners. Five eventual NBA first-round picks on team.

1978
23-8, 9-3 in ACC, first.
Postseason: NCAA, lost in first round, 68-64 to San Francisco.
Highlights: Ford, the school's career scoring leader (2,290), contributed a career-best 34 points in his final home game, an 87-83 win over Duke.

1979
23-6, 9-3 in ACC, tied for first; won ACC Tournament.
Postseason: NCAA; lost in second round after bye, 72-71 to Pennsylvania.
Highlights: UNC held the ball for first 20 minutes in season finale at Duke, as Blue Devils led 7-0 at halftime and eventually won, 47-40.

1980
21-8, 9-5 in ACC, tied for second.
Postseason: NCAA, lost in second round after bye, 78-61 in double-overtime to Texas A&M
Highlights: Third straight opening-game loss in NCAAs.

1981
29-8, 10-4 in ACC, second; won ACC Tournament.
Postseason: NCAA; lost in national championship game, 63-50 to Indiana.
Highlights: Defeated Virginia in only meeting of ACC teams in Final Four. Wing Al Wood had 39 points, the most scored in an NCAA semifinal.

1982
32-2, 12-2 in ACC, tied for first; won ACC Tournament.
Postseason: NCAA; won title, defeating Georgetown in final, 63-62.
Highlights: Top-ranked in final polls. Slowdown tactics in ACC Tournament final spur calls for shot clock. Freshman Michael Jordan hits winning jumper in NCAA title game. James Worthy scores career-high 28 points against Hoyas, goes pro.

1983
28-8, 12-2 in ACC; tied for first.
Postseason: NCAA; lost in East Regional semifinal, 82-77 to Georgia.

Highlights: Opened the season 0-2 for first time since 1929. Ended Virginia's 34-game home winning streak. Lost three straight games for first time since 1970.

28-3, 14-0 in ACC, first.
Postseason: NCAA; lost in East Regional semifinal after bye, 72-68 to Indiana.
Highlights: First undefeated ACC regular season under Smith. Top-ranked in final polls. Won 21 straight during one stretch. Michael Jordan goes pro.

27-9, 9-5 in ACC; tied for first, lost in ACC Tournament final.
Postseason: NCAA; lost in Southeast Regional final, 56-44 to Villanova.
Highlights: Lost to archrival Duke at home for first time in 19 years.

28-6, 10-4 in ACC, third.
Postseason: NCAA; lost in West Regional semifinal, 94-79 to Louisville.
Highlights: Lowest ACC finish since 1966. Top-ranked and undefeated at opening of Dean E. Smith Student Activities Center, beat third-ranked and undefeated Duke, 95-92.

32-4, 14-0 in ACC; first; lost in ACC Tournament final.
Postseason: NCAA; lost in East Regional final, 79-75 to Syracuse.
Highlights: Last team to go undefeated through an ACC season. Loss to Syracuse occasioned a firestorm of criticism directed at Smith.

27-7, 11-3 in ACC; first; lost in ACC Tournament final.
Postseason: NCAA; lost in West Regional final, 70-52 to Arizona.
Highlights: Opened the year with upset of top-ranked Syracuse. In NCAAs, stopped Loyola Marymount's 25-game win streak and made school-record 79.0 percent of field goals.

29-8, 9-5 in ACC; tied for second; won ACC Tournament.
Postseason: NCAA, lost in Southeast Regional semifinal, 92-87 to Michigan.
Highlights: First ACC Tournament title since 1982. Junior J.R. Reid goes pro.

21-13, 8-6 in ACC; tied for third.
Postseason: NCAA; lost in Midwest Regional semifinal, 96-73 to Arkansas.
Highlights: Defeated top-seeded Oklahoma in second round of NCAA. Most losses of Smith's career. Only time no Tar Heel voted All-ACC in history of league. Finished out of top 10 in polls for first time since 1980.

Deanology

1991
29-6, 10-4 in ACC; second; won ACC Tournament.
Postseason: NCAA; Final Four, lost to Kansas, 79-73.
Highlights: Routed Duke, eventual national champion, in ACC title game. Smith ejected from Final Four game against Kansas with 35 seconds to go for leaving coaches box.

1992
23-10, 9-7 in ACC; third; lost in ACC Tournament final.
Postseason: NCAA; lost in Southeast Regional semifinal, 80-73 to Ohio State.
Highlights: Lost five of last six regular-season games.

1993
34-4, 14-2 in ACC; first; lost in ACC Tournament final.
Postseason: NCAA; won title, defeating Michigan in final, 77-71.
Highlights: Sixteenth first-place ACC finish under Smith. Again won title in New Orleans.

1994
28-7, 11-5 in ACC; second; won ACC Tournament.
Postseason: NCAA; lost in East Regional second round, 75-72 to Boston College.
Highlights: Top-ranked in final regular-season AP poll. Loss to B.C. ended run of 14 consecutive Sweet 16 appearances that started in 1980.

1995
28-6, 12-4 in ACC; tied for first; lost in ACC Tournament final.
Postseason: NCAA; Final Four, lost 75-68 to Arkansas.
Highlights: Won 18 of first 19. Sophomores Jerry Stackhouse and Rasheed Wallace go pro.

1996
21-11, 10-6 in ACC; third.
Postseason: NCAA; lost in East Regional second round, 92-73 to Texas Tech.
Highlights: Smith often started three freshmen—Antawn Jamison, Vince Carter, Ademola Okulaja—for only time in his tenure.

1997
28-7, 11-5 in ACC; tied for second; won ACC Tournament.
Postseason: NCAA, Final Four, lost to Arizona, 66-58.
Highlights: Rallied from 0-3 ACC start, worst in school history. Captured 13th ACC title under Smith. Won 16 straight to reach Final Four for fourth time during 1990s, matching Duke for most appearance in decade. Smith surpassed Adolph Rupp with 877th career victory, most by a major-college coach, in 73-56 win over Colorado in East Regional second round.

SOURCES

All Dean Smith quotes in this book were gathered by Barry Jacobs except for the following:

p. 20 January 1990, Ron Morris, *Durham Morning Herald.* **p. 20** January 1972, Joe Tiede, *Raleigh News and Observer.* **p. 21** March 1988, Tucker Mitchell, *Winston-Salem Journal.* **p. 25** June 1989, Caulton Tudor, *Raleigh News and Observer.* **p. 25** June 1996, *Associated Press.* **p. 25** February 1975, Howard Owen, *The Chapel Hill Newspaper.* **p. 25** February 1978, Thad Mumau, *Fayetteville Observer.* **p. 25** February 1986, Bob Ryan, *Boston Globe.* **p. 28** March 1971, Frank Barrows, *Charlotte Observer.* **p. 28** February 1978, Don Delliquanti, *Sports Illustrated.* **p. 28** January 1972, Joe Tiede, *Raleigh News and Observer.* **p. 28** February 1978, Don Delliquanti, *Sports Illustrated.* **p. 28** March 1971, Frank Barrows, *Charlotte Observer.* **p. 30** February 1973, Russ DeVault, *Winston-Salem Journal and Sentinel.* **p. 30** February 1978, Don Delliquanti, *Sports Illustrated.* **p. 30** November 1981, Steve Schoenfeld, *Tulsa Tribune.* **p. 32** March 1984, Timothy Pritchard, *Family Weekly.* **p. 32** December 1972, Bill Brill, *Roanoke Times.* **p. 33** March 1978, Eric Siegel, *Christian Science Monitor.* **p. 33** November 1981, David Lamm, *Jacksonville Times-Union and Journal.* **p. 34** October 1996, Tim Peeler, *Durham Herald-Sun.* **p. 34** October 1977, Carl Fincke,*The Chapel Hill Newspaper.* **p. 36** January 1988, Chris Cobbs, *Raleigh News and Observer.* **p. 37** Autumn 1981, Mike Littwin, *L.A. Times.* **p. 38** Autumn 1981, Mike Littwin, *L.A. Times.* **p. 38** February 1988, *Bloomington Herald-Times.* **p. 38** December 1981, Billy Reed, *Louisville Courier-Journal.* **p. 38** November 1981, David Lamm, *Jacksonville Times-Union and Journal.* **p. 38** January 1986, *Carolina Blue.* **p. 39** March 1989, Matt Marsom, *Basketball Weekly.* **p. 43** November 1975, Keith Drum, *Durham Morning Herald.* **p. 44** February 1977, Reese Hart, *Associated Press.* **p. 46** December 1975, Bill Cronauer, *St. Petersburg Times.* **p. 46** January 1986, *Carolina Blue.* **p. 47** February 1989, Ron Green, *Charlotte Observer.* **p. 47** January 1987, John Kilgo, *Carolina Blue.* **p. 48** February 1987, Robert Markus, *Chicago Tribune.* **p. 48** March 1984, Timothy Pritchard, *Family Weekly.* **p. 49** May 1992, Tom Harris, *Raleigh News and Observer.* **p. 50** February 1975, Howard Owen, *The Chapel Hill Newspaper.* **p. 50** November 1983, Keith Drum, *Durham Morning Herald.* **p. 50** January 1964, Joe Tiede, *Raleigh News and Observer.* **p. 52** 1977, George McClelland, *Virginian-Pilot.* **p. 56** October 1983, Dean Smith, *The New York Times.* **p. 57** March 1989, Matt Marsom, *Basketball Weekly.* **p. 57** October 1982, UNC seminar on Sports and American Values. **p. 58** December 1975, Mark Whicker, *Winston-Salem Journal.* **p. 60** January 1963, Eldon Miller, *Raleigh News and Observer.* **p. 60** December 1975, Mark Whicker, *Winston-Salem Journal.* **p. 62** January 1986, *Carolina Blue.* **p. 62** March 1989, Matt Marsom, *Basketball Weekly.* **p. 64** February 1996, David Perlmutt, *Charlotte Observer.* **p. 64** August 1976, Howard Owen, *The Chapel Hill Newspaper.* **p. 71** December 1975, Mark Whicker, *Winston-Salem Journal.* **p. 71** March 1986, Bruce Martin, *Gastonia Gazette.* **p. 75** December 1987, John Schumacher, *Reno Gazette-Journal.* **p. 81** October 1982, UNC seminar on Sports and American Values. **p. 81** October 1985, Letter to UNC's Special Committee on Intercollegiate Athletics. **p. 81** May 1982, Ron Morris, *Durham Morning Herald.* **p. 83** October 1982, UNC seminar on Sports and American Values. **p. 83** March 1981, John Feinstein, *Washington Post.* **p. 83** Autumn 1979, Lee Pace, *The Daily Tar Heel.* **p. 84** October 1982, UNC seminar of Sports and

American Values. **p. 84** March 1971, Frank Barrows, *Charlotte Observer*. **p. 85** December 1972, Bill Brill, *Roanoke Times*. **p. 85** December 1993, Terry Pluto, *Akron Beacon-Journal*. **p. 86** December 1981, Billy Reed, *Louisville Courier-Journal*. **p. 86** October 1985, Letter to UNC's Special Committee on Intercollegiate Athletics. **p. 87** March 1971, Frank Barrows, *Charlotte Observer*. **p. 87** December 1976, John Montague, *Winston-Salem Sentinel*. **p. 87** January 1972, Larry Keech, *Greensboro Daily News*. **p. 87** October 1973, Frank Dascenzo, *Durham Sun*. **p. 87** October 1982, UNC Seminar on Sports and American Values. **p. 88** March 1981, John Feinstein, *Washington Post*. **p. 88** November 1981, Steve Schoenfeld, *Tulsa Tribune*. **p. 88** December 1993, Terry Pluto, *Akron Beacon-Journal*. **p. 93** Speech in Atlanta at Georgia High School Athletic Clinic. **p. 93** 1980's, Press release. **p. 94** Speech in Atlanta at Georgia High School Athletic Clinic. **p. 94** October 1982, UNC seminar on Sports and American Values. **p. 94** October 1982, UNC seminar on Sports and American Values. **p. 95** Autumn 1978, Lee Pace, *The Daily Tar Heel*. **p. 95** July 1982, Ron Green, *Charlotte News*. **p. 95** October 1982, UNC seminar on Sports and American Values. **p. 96** October 1982, UNC seminar on Sports and American Values. **p. 97** 1988, Steve Holstrom, *"The Carolina Corporation"*. **p. 97** June 1996, Ron Green, *Charlotte Observer*. **p. 98** November 1981, David Lamm, *Jacksonville Times-Union and Journal*. **p. 99** 1981, Mike Littwin, *L.A. Times*. **p. 99** March 1981, John Feinstein, *Washington Post*. **p. 100** February 1987, Robert Markus, *Chicago Tribune*. **p. 100** April 1987, Jim Laise, *Nashville Banner*. **p. 100** February 1975, Howard Owen, *The Chapel Hill Newspaper*. **p. 104** November 1981, Steve Schoenfeld, *Tulsa Tribune*. **p. 104** January 1984, John Feinstein, *Washington Post*. **p. 104** November 1989, Harry Minium, *Norfolk Virginian-Pilot*. **p. 105** March 1986, Bruce Martin, *Gastonia Gazette*. **p. 105** October 1985, Letter to UNC's Special Committee on Intercollegiate Athletics. **p. 106** October 1985, Letter to UNC's Special Committee on Intercollegiate Athletics. **p. 107** February 1975, Mark Whicker, *Winston-Salem Journal*. **p. 107** April 1985, Frank Porter Graham Lecture on Excellence at UNC. **p. 107** October 1982, UNC seminar on Sports and American Values. **p. 110** March 1981, John Feinstein, *Washington Post*. **p. 111** November 1983, Keith Drum, *Durham Morning Herald*. **p. 111** January 1971, Bill Ballenger, *Charlotte News*. **p. 111** March 1981, John Feinstein, *Washington Post*. **p. 112** January 1982, Wilt Browning, *Greensboro News and Record*. **p. 112** Autumn 1980, Bill Weronka, *Associated Press*. **p. 112** February 1987, Robert Markus, *Chicago Tribune*. **p. 112** January 1992, Wilt Browning, *Greensboro News and Record*. **p. 113** January 1992, Wilt Browning, *Greensboro News and Record*. **p. 113** March 1989, Charles Chandler, *Charlotte Observer*. **p. 113** June 1990, Bill Millsaps, *Richmond Times-Dispatch*. **p. 114** June 1990, Bill Millsaps, *Richmond Times-Dispatch*. **p. 114** June 1990, Bill Millsaps, *Richmond Times-Dispatch*. **p. 114** October 1982, Larry Keech, *Greensboro News and Record*. **p. 115** July 1982, Ron Green, *Charlotte News*. **p. 115** December 1985, Gene Frenette, *Jacksonville Times-Union*. **p. 116** March 1981, John Feinstein, *Washington Post*. **p. 116** January 1986, David Leon Moore, *USA Today*. **p. 117** 1974, Mark Whicker, *Winston-Salem Journal*. **p. 118** January 1987, Dan Collins, *Winston-Salem Journal*. **p. 119** July 1982, Ron Green, *Charlotte News*. **p. 119** Winter 1986, Paul Daugherty, *Cincinnati Enquirer*. **p. 119** Dan Collins, *Winston-Salem Journal*.